How to Understand the Sacred Scriptures

from *Clavis Scripturae Sacrae*

Matthias Flacius Illyricus

Translator
Wade R. Johnston

MAGDEBURG PRESS
SAGINAW, MICHIGAN
2011

© 2011 Magdeburg Press
8795 Ederer Road
Saginaw, MI 48609

ISBN 978-0-9821586-2-3

www.magdeburgpress.com
magdeburgpress@gmail.com

This translation is of Tractatus I, Chapters 1-4 of *Clavis Scripturae Sacrae*.

All Scripture is from the English Standard Version or is the translator's own translation, unless otherwise noted.

To Pastor Karl Vertz, for not only first teaching me the Scriptures, but teaching me to love them.

Contents

	Page
Translator's Preface	5
Introduction *Jack Kilcrease*	8
Preface	47
Causes of Difficulty in the Sacred Scriptures	48
Remedies	63
Rules for Understanding the Sacred Scriptures, Taken from the Sacred Scriptures Themselves	67
Guidelines for Reading the Sacred Scriptures, according to the Manner of Judgment We Have Assembled and Constructed	105

Translator's Preface

In any undertaking it is useful to have a proper awareness of one's shortcomings. That is especially important when translating another's words. I have done my best to be faithful to Flacius' thought and writing style, but there have been places where I have struggled to do so. Particularly in this regard, my hope is that someone more gifted—perhaps prompted by an encounter in this work with this Lutheran theologian without whom the Reformation would not have endured as it did—will improve upon my efforts and expand them, translating more of Flacius' writings, especially the full text of *Clavis Scripturae Sacrae.* While my interest in this fascinating proponent of the Reformation in Northern Europe, born and raised in Southern Europe, is surely historical, it is predominantly theological, and it is in a way personal. In Flacius we meet a Christian with whom all Christians can identify if we take the time to get to know him. Capable of great, bold, courageous acts of faith and defenses of the gospel, he also sometimes got carried away in his zeal for Christ and stumbled theologically. Yet even here he was surely driven by good intentions, and a significant case can be made that to a large extent he was misunderstood. This is not the place, however, for a theological debate. My aim is not to defend any errors into which Flacius might have fallen, but rather to indicate what about his personality as a Christian believer and theologian is so endearing. Call him what one may—and many have called him many things—Matthias Flacius was beyond a doubt sincere, while not immune to the pitfalls so common in the struggles of members of the church militant. And the Lord surely used him. His repeated and steadfast stands on Scriptures' truths bolstered those wavering under the crosses and trials that came upon evangelicals in Europe after Luther's death and largely shaped the creation and content of the Formula of Concord. For that we owe him a debt of gratitude. We do not, however, owe him any study of his writings simply for that reason. Many men and women of faith have taken breathtaking stands for the Faith throughout history, and yet their writings have not been passed down to us or have largely gone unread. No, his writings merit study for their own sake. Numerous fields of academic inquiry must acknowledge Flacius as a noteworthy figure in their development, a man possessing a truly innovative mind and remarkable diligence. My prayer is that this translation will acquaint you with one of Matthias Flacius' important works and one of the foundational works of biblical hermeneutics. As Flacius will make clear, the Bible will for the most part interpret itself, and indeed must do so, which is a truth often neglected to the Christian's detriment. The principles he enumerates here will help the student of the Bible allow the Scriptures to do just that, interpret themselves, opening up for the pious student their rich treasury of revelation and application.

Thank you to Tyler Peil, Luke Boehringer, and Mike Berg for providing advice on the editing of this translation. I appreciate the time these parish pastors took from their already busy schedules in order to aid this project. I thank their wives as well, who carry out their vocations as mothers and wives with an inspiring grace and constancy that, like that of so many pastor's wives, is seldom appreciated enough. With this in mind, let me thank Jill Peil, Sarah Boehringer, and Amanda Berg, along with my own dear wife, Tricia. Thank you also and especially to Dr. Jack Kilcrease for contributing such a fine introduction.

God is good. His saints are God's, and thus good as well in Christ, their sins forgiven, their rough edges slowly sanded by His Spirit, God's will accomplished through them in spite of their human frailty. What a wonder it is that God deigns to speak to us through men! May we see in what His saints have handed down to us the benevolent hand of our Creator and thus be driven to give even more glory to Him for such kindnesses. Innumerable Christians like Flacius have spoken and written wonderful things well before we could even form a thought in our minds. They have passed down to us a cornucopia of biblical confession. I pray that as the church in our day strives to keep its moorings it does not fail to listen to their voice, an echo of the Good Shepherd's, as much the voice of the Church today as it was hundreds of years ago. May God grant us, unless our Redeemer comes first, innumerable others like them, each with his or her own unique personality, circumstances, foibles, and insight.

Wade R. Johnston
The Epiphany of Our Lord, 2011

Introduction to the *Clavis Scripturæ Sacræ*:
The Life and Theological Contribution of Matthias Flacius Illyricus
Jack Kilcrease, Ph.D

1. Flacius' Life

Matija Vlaèiæ Ilirik (who came to be known by his Latinized named Matthias Flacius Illyricus,) was born on March 3, 1520, in Labin, Croatia.[1] "Illyricus" refers to Il-

---

[1] Jörg Baur, *Flacius- Radikale Theologie, Einsicht und Glaube, Aufsätze* (Göttingen: Vandernhoek and Ruprecht, 1978); Lauri Haikola, *Gesetz un Evangelium bei Matthias Flacius Illyricus: Eine Untersuchung zur Lutherischen Theologies vor der Konkordienformel* (Lund: Gleerup, 1952); Hans Christopher von Hase, *Die Gestalt der Kirche Luthers: Der Casus Confessionis im Kampf des Matthias Flacius gegen das Interim von 1548* (Göttingen: Vandernhoek and Ruprecht, 1940); Ivan Kordić, "Croatian Philosophers IV: Matija Vlaèiæ Ilirik – Mathias Flacius Illyricus," *Prolegomena* 4, no. 2 (2005): 219-33; Oliver K. Olson, *Matthias Flacius and the Survival of Luther's Reform* (Wiesbaden: Harrassowitz Verlag, 2002); idem, "Matthias Flacius" in *The Reformation Theologians: An Introduction to Theology in the Early Modern Period*, ed. Carter Lindberg (Malden, Mass: Blackwell, 2002), 83-94; Wilhelm Preger, *Matthias Flacius Illyricus und seine Zeit*, 2 vols. (Erlangen: Bläsing, 1859-61); J. B. Ritter, *Matthias Flacius Illyricus Leben und Tod.* (Frankfurt and Leipzig: Johann Conrad Maximilian Zeigler, 1725); August Detlev Twesten, *Matthias Flacius Illyricus, eine Verlesung. Mit Autobiorgraphischen Beilagen und einer Abhandlung über Melanchthons Verhalten zum Interim von Hermann Rössel* (Berlin: Bethage, 1844); The following are a list of Flacius' most prominent works list in Kordić, 231: *Catalogus testium veritatis, qui ante nostram aetatem reclamarunt papae*, (Basel: 1556); *Clavis Scripturae sacrae, seu De sermone Sacrarum literarum, plurimas generals regulas continens*, vol. 1 (Basel: 1567); *Clavis Scripturae sacrae, seu De sermone Sacrarum litterarum, plurimas generals Regulae continens*, vol. 2 (Basel: 1567); *De materiis metisque scientiarum, et erroribus philosophiae, in rebus divinis* (Illyrico Autore: 1563); *Disputatio de originali peccato et libero arbitrio inter Matthiam Flacium Illyricum et*

lyria, which was the name of the Roman province that became the modern nation of Croatia.[2]

Flacius did not spend much time in his native country, leaving at age sixteen in order to further his education in Venice.[3] Another contributing factor to his emigration from Croatia was likely his father's early death.[4] In Venice, Flacius received a humanist education under the instruction of Johannes Baptista Aegnatius.[5] By age 17 he intended to join the Franciscan order in order to devote himself to sacred learning.[6] However, his close relative Baldo Lupetina, a Franciscan provincial, introduced him to the theology of the Reformation movement and encouraged him not to enter into monastic life, but to pursue a humanist university career.[7]

Victorinum Strigelium, publice Vinariae per integram hebdomadam... A. 1560 initio mensis augusti, contra Papistarum et Synergistarum corruptelas habita (1562); *Gnothi seauton. De essentia originalis iustitiae et iniustitiae seu Imaginis Dei et contrariae*, (Basel: 1568); *Novum Testamentum Jesu Christi Filii Dei... cum glassa compendiaria Mathiae Flacii Illyrici Albonensis* (Frankfurt: 1659); *Paralipomena Dialectices. Libellus lectu dignissimus, et ad Dialecticam Demonstrationem certius cognoscendam, cuius etiam in Praefatione prima quaedam principia proponuntur, apprime utilis* (Basel: 1558); *Regulae et tractatus quidam de sermone sacrarum Literarum* (Magdeburg: 1551).
[2] Kordić, 219; Olson, *Matthias Flacius and the Survival of Luther's Reform*, 25; Preger, 1:13; Twesten, 3.
[3] Kordić, 219; Olson, *Matthias Flacius and the Survival of Luther's Reform*, 28-36.
[4] Preger, 1:13-4.
[5] Kordić, 220; Preger, 1:14.
[6] Kordić, 220.
[7] Olson, *Matthias Flacius and the Survival of Luther's Reform*, 32-5; Twesten, 4.

As a result, in 1539 Flacius immigrated north to Basel, Switzerland, where he studied under Sebastian Münster.[8] While there, Flacius focused on the study of Hebrew and became a leading student.[9] He also studied Greek during this period.[10] Being ever the paripatetic, he later moved on to Tübingen to the north in Baden-Württenburg and then onto Wittenberg in 1541.[11] At Wittenberg, he initially enjoyed a good relationship with leading theologian and humanist, Philip Melanchthon. Both gentlemen were at that time deeply committed to the Reformation and to the cause of humanistic learning. Having become famous as one of the greatest humanists of Germany, Melanchthon earned the nickname the *Praeceptor Germaniae*.[12] Flacius also encountered Luther and served as currier for him to communicate with other Evangelicals south of the Alps.[13] Part of the reason that Flacius had been drawn to the Reformation cause was because of his inner spiritual turmoil and his need for a divine assurance of his salvation. In fact, many believe that it was the ultimate reason why he chose to study at Wittenberg.[14] Because of the similarities between Luther's spiritual experience and Flacius' own, many have

---

[8] Olson, *Matthias Flacius and the Survival of Luther's Reform*, 35.
[9] Ibid.
[10] Ibid., 36.
[11] Twesten, 4.
[12] Olson, *Matthias Flacius and the Survival of Luther's Reform*, 41-2.
[13] Ibid., 51.
[14] Kordić,219; Olson, *Matthias Flacius and the Survival of Luther's Reform*, 48-9.

also suggested that the young Croatian humanist had a keener insight into Luther's theology than his peers.[15]

Flacius soon put down roots in Wittenberg. In 1544, he was married Elizabeth Faustus, the daughter of Pastor Michael Faustus of Dabrun.[16] He was also appointed professor of Hebrew at the university.[17] In 1546, he was awarded a master's degree. His master's thesis appropriately followed his linguistic and hermeneutical interests, and was entitled: *That Holy Scripture was Written Completely from the Beginning Not Only with Consonants, but Also With Vowel-Points.*[18]

As the title clearly indicates, Flacius held that the vowel points under Hebrew letters were original to the text and not added at a later date. Although factually untrue, this belief was long accepted in Lutheran scholastic circles, partially because this theory served a polemical purpose against certain Roman Catholic authors.[19] According to the

---

[15] Kordić, 220; Olson, *Matthias Flacius and the Survival of Luther's Reform*, 49; Twesten, 6.

[16] Olson, *Matthias Flacius and the Survival of Luther's Reform*, 53. See *Quod Sacra Scriptura Integre non Tantum Consonantibus, Sed et Inde ab Initio Scripta Fuerint, Scriptum, Olim in Promotione, ut Moris est Praeceptoribus Exhibitum* appended to *Regulae et Tractatus Quidam de Sermone Sacrarum Litrarum, ad Genuinam Multorum Difficulium Locorum Explicationem Perutiles* (Magedeburg: Michael Lotter, 1551). Olson also notes that this text made its way into the original editions of the *Clavis*.

[17] Olson, *Matthias Flacius and the Survival of Luther's Reform*, 53; Twesten, 6.

[18] Ibid. Luther admitted that the vowel marks had not been original to the text. See AE 8:141.

[19] See an example of this in Johann Gerhard, *Theological Commonplaces, Exegesis I: On the Nature of Theology and Scripture*, trans. Richard Dinda (St. Louis: Concordia Publishing House, 2005), 307-22.

latter, the absence of the vowel points in the original text opened up a basis for positing that a kind of magisterium (i.e. a divinely inspired teaching authority like the Pope) had existed in the Old Testament. The basis of this teaching authority was the knowledge of the vowel marks, something unknown to the common Jewish people.[20] The Catholic polemicists also suggested that the addition of vowel marks demonstrated the need for extra-scriptural tradition to supplement the written text.[21] This was a necessary counter-argument to the Lutheran claim that because there had been no magisterium in the Old Testament there need be none in the New.[22]

In the same year that Flacius finally earned his master's degree (1546), Luther suddenly died.[23] As a result, Melanchthon was by default placed at the head of the Wittenberg Reformation. This created several problems. First, as later events prove, Melanchthon was not temperamentally suited to function as a leader in the Reformation. The second difficulty was that he had developed theological stances at odds with those of Luther.

Melanchthon's theological differences with Luther lay in three main areas. The first was the affirmation of the freedom of the will in matters of salvation, a position which he held to after 1535.[24] The second was the Lord's Supper, wherein he had begun to develop a less realistic (though

---
[20] Ibid., 307.
[21] Ibid.
[22] This was a common Lutheran argument against Rome. See Martin Chemnitz, *Examination of the Council of Trent, Part 1*, trans. Fred Krammer (St. Louis: Concordia Publishing House, 1971), 59-63.
[23] Olson, *Matthias Flacius and the Survival of Luther's Reform*, 53.

how spiritualistic is often debated[25]) view of the Lord's Supper. The third area regarded how much should be compromised theologically for political expediency. Melanchthon, as we shall see, was much more theologically pliable than Luther. Both the issue of free will and extent of acceptable theological compromise would draw Melanchthon and Flacius into future conflicts.

Not long after Luther's death, the Emperor Charles the V began the Smalkaldic War (1546-7).[26] The war was aimed at a group of Lutheran princes known as the "Smalkaldic League," which had formed in order to promote collective security in the face of continuing Catholic

---

[24] Alister McGrath, *Iustitia Dei: A History of the Christian Doctrine of Justification* (Cambridge, UK: Cambridge University Press, 1998), 215-8; Olson, *Matthias Flacius and the Survival of Luther's Reform*, 72. Melanchthon indicates in *Loci Communes 1535* that there are three causes of conversion: the Spirit, the Word and the human will. See *Corpus Reformatorum: Philippi Melancthonis Opera Quae Supersnt Omnia*, 28 vols. Karl Bretschneider and Heinrich Bindseil, eds. (Halle: Schwetschke, 1834-1860), 23:15.

[25] Lowell Green, "The Holy Supper," in *A Contemporary Look at the Formula of Concord*, ed. Robert Preus and Wilbert Rosin (St. Louis: Concordia Publishing House, 1978), 207-11; Sachiko Kusukawa, "Melanchthon," in *The Cambridge Companion to Reformation Theology*, ed. David Bagchi and David Steinmetz (Cambridge, UK: Cambridge University Press, 2004), 60-1; Michael Rogness, *Melanchthon: Reformer without Honor* (Minneapolis: Augsburg Publishing House, 1969), 131-5. Also see Melanchthon's discussion of the Lord's Supper in Philip Melanchthon, *Melanchthon on Christian Doctrine: Loci Communes 1555*, trans. Clyde L. Manschreck (New York: Oxford University Press, 1965), 217-22. His statements here seem quite ambiguous.

[26] F. Bente, *Historical Introduction to the Lutheran Confessions* (St. Louis: Concordia Publishing House, 1965), 94-5;Olson, *Matthias Flacius and the Survival of Luther's Reform*, 68-84.

dominance in the Holy Roman Empire.[27] After defeating the Lutheran princes, Charles established the Augsburg Interim (1548) at the Diet of Augsburg.[28] The Augsburg Interim was an "interim" mainly because it was viewed as setting up a temporary framework of compromise between Catholicism and the Evangelical Churches within the Empire.[29] Charles V was in a sense, trying to find a way to please his Protestant allies who had fought against the Smalkaldic League, while maintaining his loyalty to the Papal Church.[30] Pope Paul the III had entered into an alliance with Charles in June 1548, and Charles' act of permanent compromise with the Reformation would have doubtless been viewed by him as a violation of that agreement.[31] Paul the III considered it to be within his power to decide matters of religion. He had in fact recently inaugurated the Council of Trent (beginning in 1545), whose purpose it was to define Catholic teaching and practice.[32]

---

[27] Bente, 95.
[28] Bente, 95-6; Ludwig Pastor, *The History of the Popes: From the Close of the Middle Ages*, 40 vols. trans. and eds. Frederick Ignatius Antrobus, R. F. Kerr, E. Graf, E. F. Peller (London: Trubner and Company, 1929-1953) 12:299
[29] Hans Hillerbrand, *The World of the Reformation* (Grand Rapids: Baker Book House, 1981), 105-6.
[30] Ibid., 105-6.
[31] Pastor, 12:299.
[32] Hillerbrand, *The World of the Reformation,* 105-6; idem, *The Division of Christendom: Christianity in the Sixteenth Century* (Louisville, Ky: Westminster John Knox, 2007), 275-80; Hubert Jedin, *A History of the Council of Trent*, 2 vols., trans. Ernest Graf (St. Louis: Herder, 1957-1961), 1:288-312; Carter Lindberg, *The European Reformations* (Malden, Mass: Blackwell, 1996), 350-6; Diarmaid MacCulloch, *The Reformation: A History* (New York: Penguin Books, 2003), 226-36.

Hence, the Interim was widely viewed as temporary, whether or not Charles believed it was, or harbored desires to come to an acceptable compromise for the sake of expediency.

The document constituting the Interim was composed by several theologians and contained six chapters. Its primary author was Bishop Julius von Pflug of Naumberg.[33] The Roman Catholic theologians Michael Helding, Eberhard Billick, Pedro Domenico Soto, and Pedro de Malvenda were also involved.[34] The Lutheran heretic Johann Agricola (the promoter of Antinomianism[35]) was also a contributor.[36] The goal of the document was to reestablish Roman Catholicism both *de jure* and *de facto*, while allowing cosmetic practical concessions.

In the document, the doctrine of transubstantiation was reintroduced,[37] and doctrine of justification by faith alone was rejected.[38] Similarly, the documented accepted free will as a means by which the fallen humans could cooperate with grace,[39] against the Lutheran-Augustinian emphasis on the bondage of the human will to sin after the Fall.[40]

---

[33] Pastor, 12:413.
[34] Ibid.
[35] See description in Bente, 103. Also see a full treatment in Timothy Wengert, *Law and Gospel: Philip Melanchthon's Debate with John Agricola of Eisleben over Poenitentia* (Grand Rapids: Wm. B. Eerdmans, 1997).
[36] Bente, 95; Pastor, 12:413; Preger, 1:119-20.
[37] "The Augsburg Interim, translated by Oliver K. Olson," in *Sources and Contexts of the Book of Concord*, Robert Kolb and James A. Nestingen eds. (Minneapolis: Augsburg Fortress, 2001), 163.
[38] Ibid., 152-4.
[39] Ibid., 152-3.
[40] Luther writes in the *Heidelberg Disputation*:

However, the Lutherans received small concessions, such as the reception of the Lord's Supper in both kinds.⁴¹

Melanchthon's attitude towards the document was weak and vacillating.⁴² Privately, he referred to the Interim as the "Augsburg Sphinx" and denounced its statements on justification by faith.⁴³ He even went so far as to claim that death would be easier for him than to accept it.⁴⁴ Nevertheless, he refused to speak out against it publicly.⁴⁵ Later, he worked with Maurice of Saxony (one of the victorious Protestant princes) to bring about a compromise (called the "Leipzig Interim") that exacted more theological concessions.⁴⁶

Part of the theological rationale for the second Interim document was Melanchthon's position that a Christian could accept the imposition of certain human ceremonies, without compromising the confession of the gospel.⁴⁷ Indeed, he insisted that the secular state had the right to im-

---

    Free will, after the fall, has power to do good only in a passive capacity, but it can always do evil in an active capacity. An illustration will make the meaning of this thesis clear. Just as a dead man can do something toward life only in his original capacity (*in vitam solum subiective*), so can he do something toward death in an active manner while he lives. Free will, however, is dead, as demonstrated by the dead whom the Lord has raised up, as the holy teachers of the church say. St. Augustine, moreover, proves this same thesis in his various writings against the Pelagians.

⁴¹ "The Augsburg Interim, translated by Oliver K. Olson," 178.
⁴² Bente, 98-100.
⁴³ Olson, *Matthias Flacius and the Survival of Luther's Reform*, 97.
⁴⁴ Ibid.
⁴⁵ Bente, 97-8; Olson, *Matthias Flacius and the Survival of Luther's Reform*, 99.
⁴⁶ "The Leipzig Interim, translated by Robert Kolb," in Kolb and Nestingen, 183-96.

pose anything that was *adiaphora* (a term taken from Stoic philosophy, meaning things of indifference[48]) on its citizens.[49] These compromises mainly took the form of the traditional rites and festivals of medieval Catholicism (such as the festival of *Corpus Christi*)[50] which had been previously been eliminated in lands that had accepted the Wittenberg Reformation.[51] In reality though, in spite of Melanchthon's claim to have made no compromises theologically, the document significantly undermined Lutheran teaching in several areas, not least in regard to the doctrines of grace and original sin.[52]

Flacius vigorously protested against both Interims as being a compromise of Luther's Reformation and the teachings of Scripture. Flacius insisted that no compromise in matters of *adiaphora* was possible in a time of confessional crisis (*in status confessionis*).[53] In this, he followed the Apostle Paul's teaching in the book of Galatians. Although Paul admitted that circumcision in itself was "nothing" (1 Cor 7:19, Gal 6:15), when it meant denying one's witness by publicly accepting anti-evangelical tyranny and justification by works, then it was prohibited on the grounds of the necessity of Christian witness (Gal 3). In the same way, by accepting certain Catholic ceremonies one pretended for

---

[47] Bente, 98-100; Olson, *Matthias Flacius and the Survival of Luther's Reform*, 99.
[48] Olson, "Matthias Flacius," 85.
[49] Ibid., 87.
[50] "The Leipzig Interim, translated by Robert Kolb," 194-5.
[51] Bente, 99.
[52] "The Leipzig Interim, translated by Robert Kolb," 185-91.
[53] Bente, 99-102; Olson, "Matthias Flacius," 85; Preger, 1:108-34.

the sake of political expediency to also accept their theology and therefore contradicted one's own witness to the gospel. For this reason, Flacius argued that one must follow the principle of *"in casu confessionis et scandali, nihil est adiaphoron"* ("Nothing is indifferent in a matter of confession or abuse").[54] This biblical principle of confession, as correctly expounded by Flacius, is presented in article ten of the Formula of Concord.[55]

Due to his conflict with Melanchthon and others in his party, Flacius moved to Magdeburg in 1549.[56] He energetically supported the cause of the city of Magdeburg, which had continued its resistance against the Emperor in the face of terrible odds.[57] In 1550, he offered the Magdeburg Confession as a sort of formula of concord in order to quell the strife that had arisen among the Lutheran Churches as a result of the Interim.[58] Melanchthon did not accept this confession though, because it held to Flacius' view of *adiaphora* and because it rejected a role for free will to play in salvation.[59]

During his time in Magdeburg, Flacius also began his work in consultation with other scholars on the *Magdeburg*

---

[54] Olson, "Matthias Flacius," 85. Preger, 1:142.
[55] SD, X; Ep, X in *Concordia Triglotta: The Symbolic Books of the Evangelical Lutheran Church*, ed. and trans. W. H. T. Dau and F. Bente (St. Louis: Concordia Publishing House, 1921), 829-31, 1053-63.
[56] Olson, *Matthias Flacius and the Survival of Luther's Reform*, 147.
[57] See theological background to this in Oliver K. Olson, "Theology of Revolution: Magdeburg 1550-1551," *The Sixteenth Century Journal* 3 (1972): 50-79.
[58] Olson, "Matthias Flacius," 87.
[59] Ibid.

Centuries.⁶⁰ The *Centuries* was the first modern unified history of the Church. Werner Elert opined that it formed the basis of all modern Church history.⁶¹ Its name derives from its organization of Church history into units of one-hundred years.⁶² It spades the time from the birth of Christ to the sixteenth century.⁶³ Flacius' work was revolutionary in many respects. One of its most significant features was that it was overwhelmingly based on primary sources. Additionally, unlike most medieval and early modern Catholic histories, it discounted the legendary accounts of the saints.⁶⁴ Even after Flacius had left Magdeburg, he retained editorial control over the development of the work.⁶⁵

---

⁶⁰ Olson, *Matthias Flacius and the Survival of Luther's Reform*, 265-65; Preger, 2:416-68; Twesten, 14-17. The official and full title is: *Ecclesiastica Historia, integram Ecclesiae Christi ideam, quantum ad Locum, Propagationem, Persecutionem, Tranquillitatem, Doctrinam, Hæreses, Ceremonias, Gubernationem, Schismata, Synodos, Personas, Miracula, Martyria, Religiones extra Ecclesiam, et statum Imperii politicum attinet, secundum singulas Centurias, perspicuo ordine complectens: singulari diligentia et fide ex vetustissimis et optimis historicis, patribus, et aliis scriptoribus congesta: Per aliquot studiosos et pios viros in urbe Magdeburgica.* See a fuller description of their development in Gregory Lyon, "Baudouin, Flacius, and the Plan for the Magdeburg Centuries," *Journal of the History of Ideas* 64, no. 2 (2003): 253-272; And also see Ronald Diner, "The Magdeburg Centuries: A Bibliothecal and Historiographical Analysis," (Unpublished Dissertation, Harvard Divinity School, 1978).
⁶¹ Werner Elert, *The Structure of Lutheranism: The Theology and Philosophy of Life of Lutheranism Especially in the Sixteenth and Seventeenth Centuries*, vol. 1, trans. Walter A. Hansen (St. Louis: Concordia Publishing House, 1962), 485
⁶² Olson, *Matthias Flacius and the Survival of Luther's Reform*, 262-3.
⁶³ Ibid.
⁶⁴ Olson, *Matthias Flacius and the Survival of Luther's Reform*, 256-7; Elert, 488.
⁶⁵ Olson, *Matthias Flacius and the Survival of Luther's Reform*, 298.

Around the same time, Flacius also began a dispute with Andreas Osiander over the question of forensic justification. He insisted on Luther and Melanchthon's forensic understanding the person's righteousness before God, whereas Osiander conflated justification with *unio mystica*.[66] Flacius also used the debate as an occasion to develop explicitly the distinction between Christ's "active" (his obedience to the law) and "passive" (his payment of sin on behalf of the human race) righteousness in his work *Con-*

---

[66] Bente, 152-9; I. A. Dorner, *History of the Development of the Doctrine of the Person of Christ*, 5 vols., trans. William Alexander, D. W. Simon, and Patrick Fairbairn (Edinburgh: T & T Clark, 1872-1882), 4:107-15; idem, *History of Protestant Theology, Particularly in Germany*, 2 vols., trans. George Robson and Sophia Taylor (Edinburgh: T & T Clark, 1871), 1:353-69; Justo González, *A History of Christian Thought*, 3 vols. (Nashville: Abingdon Press, 1987), 3:114-8; Henry Hamann, "The Righteousness of Faith before God," in Preus and Rosin, 137-62; Robert Kolb, "Historical Background of the Formula of Concord," in Preus and Rosin, 36-41; Carl Lawrenz, "On Justification, Osiander's Doctrine of the Indwelling of Christ," in *No Other Gospel: Essays in Commemoration of the 400th Anniversary of the Formula of Concord, 1580-1980*, ed. Arnold Koelpin (Milwaukee: Northwestern Publishing House, 1980), 149-74; McGrath, 213; Olson, "Matthias Flacius," 86; Jaroslav Pelikan, *The Christian Tradition: A History of the Development of Doctrine*, 5 vols. (Chicago: University of Chicago Press, 1971- 1989), 4:150-2; Preger, 1:205-98; Albrecht Ritschl, *A Critical History of the Christian Doctrine of Justification and Reconciliation*, trans. John Black (Edinburgh: Edmonton and Douglas, 1872), 214-33; Otto Ritschl, *Dogmengeschichte des Protestantismus*, 4 vols. (Göttingen: Vandenhoeck and Ruprecht, 1927), 2:455-88; Reinhold Seeberg, *Text-Book of the History of Doctrines*, 2 vols. trans. Charles Hay (Grand Rapids: Baker Book House, 1977), 2:369-74; Olli-Pekka Vainio, *Justification and Participation in Christ: The Development of the Lutheran Doctrine of Justification from Luther to the Formula of Concord (1580)* (Leiden: Brill, 2008), 95-118. Also see Andreas Osiander, *Von dem Einigen Mittler Jhesu Christo un Rechtfertigung des Glaubens Benkenntnus* (Königsberg: 1551).

cerning Righteousness vs. Osiander (1552).⁶⁷ Much like his view of *adiaphora*, Flacius' view of justification found widespread support and is today enshrined in the third article of the Formula of Concord.⁶⁸

In 1557, Flacius left Magdeburg and became a professor of New Testament at the University of Jena, where he remained active in ecclesiastical politics. ⁶⁹ Jena became a hotbed of "Gnesio" (Genuine) Lutheranism, which was supported by Duke Johann Friedrich the Middler.⁷⁰ For this reason, Flacius gained some political influence. In the same year Flacius arrived at Jena, he was able to frustrate an inappropriate religious compromise by the Prince with the Emperor at Worms.⁷¹

---

⁶⁷ Heinrich Schmid, *The Doctrinal Theology of the Evangelical Lutheran Church*, trans. Charles Hay and Henry Jacobs (Minneapolis: Augsburg Publishing House, 1961), 354. Flacius writes:
> The justice of God, as revealed in the Law, demands of us, poor, unrighteous, disobedient men, two items of righteousness. The first is, that we render to God complete satisfaction for the transgression and sin already committed; the second, that we thenceforth be heartily and perfectly obedient to His Law if we wish to enter life. If we do not thus accomplish this, it threatens us with eternal damnation. And therefore the essential justice of God includes us under sin and the wrath of God . . . Therefore the righteousness of the obedience of Christ, which He rendered to the Law for us, consists in these two features, viz., in His suffering and in perfect obedience to the commands of God.

Also see discussion in Albrecht Ritschl, 219-221, 226-29.
⁶⁸ SD III and Ep III in *Concordia Triglotta*, 791-797, 971-37.
⁶⁹ Olson, *Matthias Flacius and the Survival of Luther's Reform*, 323; Twesten, 17.
⁷⁰ Olson, "Matthias Flacius," 87.
⁷¹ Olson, "Matthias Flacius," 87; Preger, 2:104-80.

At this time, Flacius entered into disputes with followers of Philip Melanchthon, who had come to dominate the University of Wittenberg.[72] In particular, Melanchthon's synergism became a hot topic of discussion. In 1560, Flacius was drawn into a fateful public debate with the prominent Philippist Victorinus Strigel at Weimar in the presence of the local Duke.[73] In order explain to his audience and opponents the capacity of free will to cooperate with grace after the Fall, Strigel used an Aristotelian distinction between "substance"[74] and "accidents."[75] According to his description, the human "substance" (that is, what in essence it means to be human) had not been changed by the Fall.[76] Rather, what had changed were its "accidents" (the particular individual qualities of a thing, that inhere in the substance without changing its essence).[77] Although human free will's quality had changed by being weakened by sin,

---

[72] Olson, "Matthias Flacius," 87.

[73] Bente, 144-5; Dorner, *History of Protestant Theology*, 1:370-83; González, 3:124-5; Richard Klann, "Original Sin," in Preus and Rosin, 115-7; Robert Kolb, *Bound Choice, Election, and the Wittenberg Theological Method: From Martin Luther to the Formula of Concord* (Grand Rapids: Wm. B. Eerdmans, 2005), 118-20; Also by the same author: "Historical Background to the Formula of Concord," 29-33; Kordić, 229. Olson, "Matthias Flacius," 87; Pelikan, 4:142-4; Preger, 2:310-412; Otto Ritschl, 2:430-54; Seeberg, 2:367-9; Twesten, 20-22; Heinrich Vogel, "On Original Sin, The Flacian Aberration" in Koelpin, 126-31.

[74] Aristotle, *Metaphysics* 1.1-3 in *The Metaphysics*, trans. David Bostock (New York: Oxford University Press, 1994), 1-4.

[75] Aristotle, *Metaphysics* 1.4, Ibid., 4-6.

[76] Bente, 146; Kolb, *Bound Choice*, 118-20.

[77] Bente, 145-6; Kolb, *Bound Choice*, 118-20. Vogel, 127-8.

it did not mean that it had been essentially eliminated and, therefore, could be activated by grace.[78]

In the heat of the debate, when asked by Strigel if original sin was a substance or accident, Flacius angrily insisted that since sin defined humanity after the Fall, it was proper to call it a substance.[79] In later writings, Flacius would go so far as to claim that not only had humanity lost the image of God (*imago dei*) because of the Fall, but that the image had been replaced by the image of the Devil (*imago diabolii*).[80]

Flacius' use of the word "substance" to describe original sin was problematic for several reasons. First, taken literally, it endangered the doctrine of creation. If God is the author of the human substance, then it must be good. Obviously, Scripture clearly teaches this in Genesis 1 with the constant refrain "it was very good." If one posits that the essence of humanity had in fact become evil because of the Fall, God (who is the author of every essence) would become the author of evil. Alternatively, one could claim that Satan was the author of this substance, but this again would deny God's sole agency as creator and also make Satan a second God.[81] Thirdly, Flacius' way of speaking also raised issues regarding the Incarnation. If Christ took on human nature, Flacius' statements would logically sug-

---

[78] Bente, 144; Kolb, *Bound Choice*, 118-20; Vogel, 128-9.
[79] Bente, 144; Kolb, *Bound Choice*, 118-20; Preger, 2:214; Twesten, 26; Vogel, 128-9.
[80] Haikola, 118-28; Pelikan, 4:142-4; Vainio, 114.
[81] See summary of these arguments in Robert Jenson, *Thinking the Human: Resolutions of Difficult Notions* (Grand Rapids: Wm B. Eerdmans, 2003), 62-4

gest that he either had to become a sinner (since human nature had been so transformed by the Fall) or on the other hand, by taking on sinless human nature he took on a nature alien to us. Consequently, he would not have been able to represent and redeem other fallen humans.

It should be noted that Flacius in actuality did not mean the term "substance" in the sense that others imputed to him or in the way that the term was typically used in Aristotelian philosophy.[82] In using the expression, he merely wanted to emphasize, as Luther had before him, that humans after the Fall were bound to sin and relationally defined by it in the eyes of God (*coram deo*).[83] For him, there was no spark of free will capable of being activated by grace left over from the Fall, as Strigel suggested.[84] Therefore, in a sense, although it is commonly said that the "Flacian heresy" is condemned by the Formula of Concord article one,[85] only Flacius' choice of words not his actual confession of faith was rejected. Flacius' understanding of human moral agency after the Fall was in fact accepted by the Confessors, while Melanchthon and Strigel's synergism was rejected. The Confessors merely rejected Flacius' use of language.

As a result of his debate with Strigel, a public furor began among theologians regarding Flacius' teaching.[86]

---

[82] Bente, 147; Vogel, 134-5.

[83] See WA 42:47. Luther here uses language about Adam's condition after the Fall that is almost identical language to Flacius here: "*Haec et similia mala sunt imago Diaboli, qui ea nobis.*"

[84] Bente, 145-6.

[85] SD I and Ep I; *Concordia Triglotta,* 779-85, 859-879.

[86] Kolb, *Bound Choice,* 120-7; Vogel, 135-40.

His stubborn refusal to change his language finally earned him ecclesiastical censure in 1562.[87] Resisting it, he fled Jena and ended up in Regensburg in Austria, where he attempted unsuccessfully to found a university to disseminate the Wittenberg Reformation to the Slavic countries.[88] Next he was called to Antwerp, where he was called to advise the Lutheran community there.[89] Flacius played an important role in the formation of their liturgical practice and ecclesiastical governance.[90]

Unfortunately, war in the Netherlands forced Flacius to flee to Strasbourg, where his theological views on original sin earned him exile again.[91] He proceeded on to Frankfurt where he was received by the superintendent Johannes Marbach.[92] It was also during this period that he composed and published the *Clavis Scriptura Sacræ* (1567). Again in 1573, once his views became known, he was ordered into exile.[93] Nevertheless, the prioress Catharina von Meerfeld of the Convent of White Ladies secretly allowed him to remain in the city and she hid him and his family for the next two years.[94] Flacius eventually became sick and died on March 11, 1575. He had just turned 55 years old.[95]

---

[87] Olson, "Matthias Flacius," 87.
[88] Kordić, 220; Preger 2:228-84; Twesten, 23-5.
[89] Olson, "Matthias Flacius," 87; Preger, 2:285-94; Twesten, 25.
[90] Olson, "Matthias Flacius," 87.
[91] Preger, 2:296-301; Twesten, 26.
[92] Preger, 2:298, 2:307-9; Twesten, 29.
[93] Preger, 2:517.
[94] Ibid.
[95] Ibid., 2:526-7; Twesten, 30.

2. Flacius' Theological Hermeneutics: A Faithful Continuation of Luther and Melanchthon's Legacy

Flacius' *Clavis Scripturæ Sacræ* (1567) reveals him to be a student of both Luther and Melanchthon. It must be born in mind that the shift in thinking that led to the Reformation was not just one of doctrinal orientation, but also one of methodology. This shift was not something that came out of the blue, but had antecedents in both the humanist and late scholastic traditions. Flacius follows Luther and Melanchthon's methodological shifts in his *Clavis* in several important ways. First, he emphasizes with Luther the need to focus on the literal sense of Scripture and also follows his distinction between its internal and external clarity. Secondly, Flacius follows Melanchthon by his insistence on the need for the rhetorical criticism of Scripture and endorsement of the *loci* method for interpreting the Bible's dogmatic content. Finally, Flacius agrees with Luther that the Bible is best understood when it is read according to the threefold practice of prayer, meditation, and trial/suffering (*oratio, medatatio, tentatio*).

As we noted above, the first area of continuity with Luther is Flacius' insistence on a single, literal sense of Scripture (*sensus literalis*). This stands in contrast to the mainstream of medieval theology's insistence on the fourfold sense of Scripture. Regarding this question of the senses of Scripture, Flacius writes:

> The reader should be content to lay hold of the simple and genuine sense of the Sacred Scriptures, and especially of that place which he is reading at the time, and he should not chase after any kinds

> of shadows or eagerly pursue dreams about allegories or higher meaning [*anagogia*], except when it is manifestly an allegory and the literal sense is otherwise unsuitable or absurd.[96]

Here Flacius claims that we should (unless we are compelled otherwise by the text's own claims about itself) accept the literal, historical-grammatical meaning of the words. As he states elsewhere, this literal meaning is both the grammatical meaning of the text and the meaning of the words within the overall organic structure of the text. He is critical of certain Roman Catholic authors who attempt to piece together statements of Scripture without attention to context. According to Flacius, they do so only to vindicate their own non-biblical doctrinal systems.[97] Against this Roman Catholic tendency Flacius argues that the Bible must be considered as a body[98] and must be read in light of its organic unity.[99]

For this reason, the "literal sense" should not be identified with literalism or perhaps one might say "letterism."

---

[96] Flacius, *How to Understand the Sacred Scriptures*, 106.

[97] Flacius, 117-118. Flacius writes:
> The papists and the sophists have sinned most grievously and perniciously against this precept. They have very rarely seen to the reading of the Sacred Scriptures, and when they have been read, have only plucked certain little sentences at their discretion and, even more, have connected them to each according to their good pleasure like a young girl gathering flowers in the meadow according to her will and whimsy and playfully weaving them together into a wreath or something else.

[98] Flacius, 107; Bengt Hägglund, "Pre-Kantian Hermeneutics in Lutheran Orthodoxy," *Lutheran Quarterly* 20, no. 3 (2006): 321; Kordić, 229.

[99] Flacius, 79; Hägglund, 320; Kordić, 228-9.

"The LORD is my rock" (Ps 18:2) does not mean that God is a piece of stone. Rather, the literal sense is the divinely intended meaning of Scripture as it pertains to its concrete historical setting.[100] Hans Frei has best described this as a harmony of the grammatical and historical meaning of a text within its place in the overall context of the Bible and its narrative.[101] This sense does not reduce texts to their historical contexts without reference to God's overall plan for history or his supernatural agency, as the term "literal sense" later came to mean in the eighteenth and nineteenth centuries.[102] For this reason, the literal sense does not exclude typology[103] or rectilinear prophecy.[104] Each event of

---

[100] Thomas Aquinas, *Summa Theologiae*, pt. 1, q. 1, art. 10, in *The Summa in 5 Vols*. trans. Fathers of the English Dominican Province (Notre Dame: Ave Maria Press, 1948), 1:7. Aquinas states: ". . . the literal sense is that which the author intends and . . . the author of Holy Writ is God . . ."

[101] Hans Frei, *The Eplipse of Biblical Narrative: A Study in Eighteenth and Nineteenth Century Hermeneutics* (New Haven: Yale University Press, 1974), 17-46.

[102] Ibid., 86-104.

[103] Typology is different than allegory. Allegory is vertical and makes one thing a metaphor for another. The heavenly type can be seen through the earthly form. Typology is horizontal and draws an analogical similarity between events as the compromise a single narrative of salvation. If God is the single agent of the history of redemption, then his earlier actions must harmoniously prefigure his later ones.

[104] It is also possible that it may include allegory to a limited extent. Flacius appears to be somewhat inconsistent on this point. Benjamin Mayes notes that although Flacius was skeptical of allegory (he repeatedly says so in the *Clavis*), he went so far as to include the highly allegorical *libruni formulnrunl spiritalis intelligntiae* by Eucherius of Lyons in his first edition of the *Clavis*. See footnote 30 in Benjamin Mayes, "The Mystical Sense of Scripture According to Johann Jacob Rambach" *Concordia Theological Quarterly* 72, no. 1 (2008):49.

salvation history is brought about by God, who is also the author of the text of the Bible. All formed together a harmonious pattern of meaning. Hence, all events in salvation history must be read as mutually interpreting. One event or text does not simply exist by itself, but only gains meaning in the overall structure that God has created.[105]

In his adherence to the literal sense of Scripture, Flacius is a true student of Luther. Samuel Preus has demonstrated[106] Luther's theological revolution began with a shift from the fourfold sense (still evident in his early Psalms commentaries) to an exclusive emphasis on the literal sense.[107] Luther's preference for the literal sense was in and of itself not unprecedented. In making this shift he simply followed earlier medieval interpreters who relied on the literal sense such as Nicolas of Lyra.[108] Luther's move was unique only in the sense that his shift to the literal sense became a vehicle for his eventual recognition that the Bible centers on God's fulfillment in historical time of his literal promises. Thus, according to Preus, because Luther understood the Old Testament as a concrete, literal promise about salvation coming in the future (rather than a mystical

---

[105] See a modern argument for this reading of the Bible in Peter Leithart, *Deep Exegesis: The Mystery of Reading Scripture* (Waco, TX: Baylor University Press, 2009) and idem, *A Son to Me: An Exposition of 1 and 2 Samuel* (Moscow, ID: Canon Press, 2003), 9-24.
[106] Samuel Preus, *From Shadow to Promise: Old Testament Interpretation from Augustine to the Young Luther* (Cambridge, Mass: Harvard University Press, 1969).
[107] Ibid., 182.
[108] See discussion in Steven Ozment, *The Age of Reform, 1250-1550: An Intellectual and Religious History of Medieval and Reformation Europe* (New Haven: Yale University Press, 1980), 67-72.

shadow of some transcendental realities in heaven) he was prepared for the later insights that came about in the Reformation breakthrough.[109] For Luther, in the Old Testament, people had awaited the literal fulfillment of promises regarding the Messiah; just modern Christians awaited Christ's return in glory.[110]

According to Oswald Bayer, the Reformation breakthrough was itself related to the literal sense. The breakthrough, claims Bayer, was Luther's realization that the words "I absolve you" (*ego te absolve!*) were identical with God's own presence with and in the Word enacting what the Word promised.[111] This is why, although his preference for the literal sense pre-existed the Reformation breakthrough, it remained a mainstay of his theology throughout his whole life, as his comments in the Genesis commentary (1535-45) show.[112] If the reception of justification and the absolute assurance of salvation were identical with the event of the proclamation of forgiveness, then God himself must be thought of as donating himself, in, under, and with the Word of absolution. Unlike the allegorical reading of Scripture, God's literal demands and literal promises do not echo any higher reality. The law literally works condemnation on sinners. The gospel literally gives what it promises when received by faith. For this reason, Luther's emphasis

---

[109] Samuel Preus, 226-7.
[110] Ibid., 212-225.
[111] Oswald Bayer, *Martin Luther's Theology: A Contemporary Interpretation*, trans. Thomas Trapp (Grand Rapids: Wm. B. Eerdmans, 2008), 52-3.
[112] AE 2:150-64; 3:27-31, 34.

(shared by Flacius[113]) on law and gospel stands in harmony with their emphasis on the literal sense of Scripture.

Such a way of conceptualizing divine agency through the earthly medium of Scripture has other implications in Luther's theology. For example, it quite clearly parallels Luther's own Christological teaching, wherein as a result of the hypostatic union there is a communication of the fullness of divine glory to the flesh of Jesus (the Lutheran theologian and co-author of the Formula of Concord, Martin Chemnitz, would later call this the *genus maiestaticum*). [114] Indeed, as Luther would write of Jesus in *A Mighty*

---

[113] Flacius, 74-75; Flacius writes regarding John 3:16: "There are two kinds of doctrine, therefore: law and gospel. Both of these are indeed opposed to each other according to their nature. The former certainly offers salvation to none except those worthy and righteous. The latter, however, only offers salvation to the most unworthy."

[114] See discussion in Johann Baier, *Compendium Theologiae Positivae*, 2 vols., ed. C. F. W. Walther (Grand Rapids: Emmanuel Press, 2005-2006), 2:52-70; Martin Chemnitz, *The Two Natures in Christ*, trans. J. A. O Preus (St. Louis: Concordia Publishing House, 1971), 241-7; Adolf Hoenecke, *Evangelical Lutheran Dogmatics*, 4 vols. Trans. Joel Fredrich, James L. Langebartels, Paul Prange, and Bill Tackmier (Milwaukee: Northwestern Publishing House, 1999-2009), 3:89-99; Nicolaus Hunnius, *Epitome Credendorum*, trans. Paul Gottheil (Nuremburg: U. E. Sebald, 1847), 104-7; Leonard Hütter, *Compendium Locorum Theologicorum Ex Scripturis Sacris et Libro Concordiae:Lateinisch-Deutsch-Englisch*, 2 vols., trans. Henry Jacobs (Stuttgart-Bad Cannstatt: Friedrich Frommann Verlag, 2006), 2:928-32; Gerhard, 203-87; A. L. Graebner, *Outline of Doctrinal Theology* (St. Louis: Concordia Publishing House, 1949), 109-10; Edward Koehler, *A Summary of Christian Doctrine: A Popular Presentation of the Teachings of the Bible* (St. Louis: Concordia Publishing House, 2006), 91-2; John Theodore Mueller, *Christian Dogmatics* (St. Louis: Concordia Publishing House, 2003), 275-83; Francis Pieper, *Christian Dogmatics*, 3 vols. (St. Louis: Concordia Publishing House, 1951-1953), 2:152-242; John Schaller, *Biblical Christology: A Study in Lutheran Dogmatics* (Milwaukee: Northwestern Publishing House,

Fortress is Our God: "There is no other God!"[115] In other words, God's full reality has been donated to the man Jesus and we will look for God nowhere else. This is the same logic behind his zealous defense of the real presence against Zwingli.[116] The nature of the gospel means God's unilateral surrender to us in his self-binding in the gospel. This surrender means that God makes himself completely available to us in the flesh of Jesus mediated to faith in, under, and with the Word of the Bible and the Sacraments. In this scheme, humans are therefore always passive receivers of God's address of law and gospel (*vita passiva*).

The fourfold concept of Scripture also parallels the medieval concept of salvation and the divine-human relationship. The fourfold sense of Scripture[117] understood the Bible as having a literal (historical-grammatical),[118] moral (moral teaching),[119] allegorical (wherein doctrines were capable of being metaphorically described using different

---

1981), 68-78; Schmid, 314-5; Vainio, 141. Flacius does share Luther's belief n the communication of attributes, though he emphasizes it less. See comment in Vainio, 116, footnote 96.

[115] AE 53:285. The translation actually reads: "And God but him is none." This is a bit of a rough translation. I have paraphrased the line rather than given a direct citation or translation.

[116] See description in Hermann Sasse, *This is My Body: Luther's Contention for the Real Presence in the Sacrament of the Altar* (St. Louis: Concordia Publishing House, 2003).

[117] See brief description in Pelikan 3:40-1. See Aquinas' summary in *Summa Theologiae*, pt. 1, q. 1, art. 10 , in *Summa,* 1:7.

[118] See discussion in Henri De Lubac, *Medieval Exegesis: The Four Senses of Scripture*, 3 vols., trans. Mark Sebanc, and E. M. Macierowski (Grand Rapids: Wm. B. Eerdmans, 1998-2009), 2:41-82; Pelikan, 100.

[119] De Lubac, 2:127-78.

events and persons in salvation history),[120] and anagogical (that is, typological of eschatological and heavenly realities) senses.[121]

Broadly speaking, in medieval theology, the human person is given grace and thereby is able to move closer and closer to God in a kind of ascension through merit.[122] The "wayfarer" (*viator*) does this by leaving earthly things behind through contemplating the divine (faith) and accumulating merit (love).[123] Paralleling this scheme of salvation, for medieval interpretation, the text has an earthly jumping off point (literal sense). It also has a means of ascending to the heavenly realm through true knowledge of Gods' transcendental reality (allegorical sense) and accumulating merit through good behavior (moral sense).[124] Through this, one finally reaches heavenly existence (the anagogical sense). In this conception, God does not unilaterally donate himself to sinners in his literal promises, but rather through the Word he gives temporal echoes of his heavenly reality so that humans may use them as vehicles of ascension. In other words, it posits the law and not the gospel of God's own self-donation is a way to salvation. Humans are active and not passive.

---

[120] De Lubac, 2:83-126; Pelikan, 3:39-40.
[121] De Lubac, 2:179-226.
[122] McGrath, 100-9.
[123] See discussion of Thomas Aquinas' view of the virtues faith and love in Aquinas, *Summa Theologiae* pt. I-II, q. 62, art. 1-4, in *Summa*, 2:851-3.
[124] McGrath, 109.

Because the Bible is the Word of God[125] and possesses a spiritual reality present in, under, and with its literal grammatical sense, then the text must possess clarity so that faith may receive its promises. Regarding the clarity of the Bible, Luther posited that there were two types: internal and external. As we shall see, Flacius also posits these two forms of clarity.

Luther most forcefully makes this distinction in his work *Bondage of the Will* (1525). Beyond the question of free will and predestination, Luther wished to counter Erasmus' claims that Scripture was ambiguous, particularly regarding the question at hand.[126] For Erasmus, the text of

---

[125] Flacius., 70-71. Flacius writes:
> The summary of Scripture, therefore, is these two syllogisms. The first and most important syllogism of the Old Testament is this: *Whatever God says is true.* That needs no proving. It is indeed the foundational principle of all theology, deserving of the assent of every creature. "Our words," say Moses and the prophets, "are the words of God, and He has spoken through us. Therefore our words and writings are most true, whether concerning creation and the fall, or the blessed Seed and the Messiah."

See discussion of Flacius' view of inspiration in Otto Ritschl, 1:142-53. Ritschl shows that Flacius holds to verbal inspiration and attributes to him the origination of this doctrine. Richard Muller shows that the idea of direct divine involvement in production of the Scriptures is not new in Flacius, but part of the biblical and ecumenical doctrine of the Church-catholic. See Richard Muller, *Post-Reformation Reformed Dogmatics: The Rise and Development of Reformed Orthodoxy ca. 1520 to ca. 1725*, 4 vols. (Grand Rapids: Baker Academic, 2003), 3:38-94.

[126] Interestingly enough, without the Holy Spirit as the cause of the clarity of Scripture, this tends to be the position of those who believe in free will. In Roman Catholicism, since everyone has free will to either accept the correct meaning of Scripture or corrupt it he Bible's meaning is ambiguous. This Scripture's ambiguity necessitates the existence of the papacy. This position was also held in Arminianism, where in its

Scripture was merely a dead letter, read by rational and autonomous humans. Erasmus' anthropology was quite close to that of Strigel, whom Flacius opposed. Because of his view of human nature, Erasmus assumed that human beings as free-agents are capable of manipulating texts as they choose.[127] In evaluating different interpretations, one

---

seventeenth century incarnation, tolerance in the doctrinal matters was urged. See a description of the early Arminian position in Kevin Vahoozer, *Is There Meaning in This Text?: The Bible, The Reader, and the Morality of Literary Knowledge* (Grand Rapids: Zondervan, 1998), 297-9.

[127] For a description of Luther's debate with Erasmus see the follow sources: Roland Baintain, *Here I Stand: A Life of Martin Luther* (Nashville: Abingdon, 1978), 195-8; Bayer, 83-5, 187-90; Bente, 209-25; Martin Brecht, *Martin Luther*, 3 vols. (Minneapolis: Fortress Press, 1985-1993), 2:213-38; Dorner, *History of Protestant Theology*, 1:202-19; Gerhard Forde, *The Captivation of the Will: Luther vs. Erasmus on Freedom and Bondage*, ed. Steven Paulson (Grand Rapids: Wm. B. Eerdmans, 2005); Eric Gritsch, *Martin: God's Court Jester: Luther in Retrospect* (Philadelphia: Fortress Press,1983), 61-3; James Kittelson, *Luther the Reformer: The Story of the Man and His Career* (Minneapolis: Augsburg Publishing House, 1986), 203-6; Kolb, *Bound Choice*, 11- 66; Julius Köstlin, *The Theology of Luther in Its Historical Development and Inner Harmony*, 2 vols., trans. Charles Hay (Philadelphia, Lutheran Publication Society, 1897), 1:475-97; Harry McSorley, *Luther: Right or Wrong?, An Ecumenical-Theological Study of Luther's Major Work, The Bondage of the Will* (New York and Minneapolis: The Newman Press and Augsburg Publishing House, 1969), 277-354; Bernhard Lohse, *Martin Luther's Theology: Its Historical and Systematic Development*, trans. Roy Harrisville (Minneapolis: Fortress Press, 1999), 16-8; Richard Marius, *Martin Luther: The Christian between God and Death* (Cambridge, Mass: Harvard University Press, 1999), 442-68; McGrath, 202-3; Heiko Oberman, *Luther: Man Between God and the Devil*, trans. Eileen Walliser-Schwarzbart (New Haven: Yale University Press, 1989), 211-220; E. G. Schwiebert, *Luther and His Times: The Reformation from a New Perspective* (St. Louis: Concordia Publishing House, 1950), 683-94; David Steinmetz, *Luther in Context* (Bloomington: Indiana University Press,1986), 23-31.

could not be certain to what extent the interpreter's freely chosen decisions regarding how to read the text had played into perceived meaning. Erasmus also goes to great pains to show that one can simply pile up biblical quotations for or against a given position. Which side one will choose is ultimately arbitrary and irrelevant, since doctrine was mainly viewed by him as an abstraction. Hence, one needed to be skeptical of overly dogmatic readings of texts and focus instead on the moral content of the text, as Erasmus did in his own personal writings.[128]

Luther, on the contrary, believed that humans were passive subjects of God's address of law and gospel.[129] The text was clear because God was his own exegete. The clarity of the text was not due to the rational and autonomous efforts of human beings.[130] Bound sinners without Christ and the Spirit never understand the Scriptures properly because their minds, distorted by sin, cannot perceive the true meaning.[131] The Scripture's center is Jesus Christ.[132] He is the one who opens our ears and allows us to hear true meaning of the Bible.[133] Through faith in him, worked by

---

[128] See for example, Erasmus, *The Enchiridion*, trans. Raymond Himelick (Bloomington: Indiana University, 1963).
[129] AE 33:132-8.
[130] See Forde, 23-30, on scriptural clarity. Also see a good, but not perfect, discussion of Luther's view of the clarity of Scripture in Vitor Westhelle, "Luther on the Authority of Scriptures," *Lutheran Quarterly* 19, no. 4 (2005): 373-91.
[131] AE 33:27-8.
[132] AE 33:26.
[133] Bayer, *Luther's Theology*, 68-74. Bayer describes the Church in Luther's theology as a communion of hearers.

the power the Spirit, the true meaning of the Bible becomes evident. This is the inner clarity of the Bible.[134]

Flacius agrees with Luther that the Bible is only understandable in light of Christ and the Holy Spirit:

> When we are converted to Christ, then the veil is taken off of our heart and also from the Scriptures, not only because we are illumined with spiritual light, but also because we grasp the scope and argument of all of Scripture, namely, the Lord Jesus, with His suffering and benevolent service (2 Corinthians 3:16). For the end of the law is Christ. That alone is the pearl of great price and when we have found it in this field of the Lord we then go about our life well satisfied.[135]

The name "*Clavis*" itself bears witness to Flacius emphasis on inner clarity. As Bengt Hägglund notes, the name "*Clavis*" or "key" is a reference to Christ's role in Revelation chapter five as the one who is capable of opening the scroll with the seven seals.[136] Indeed as Flacius

---

[134] AE 33:25-8.

[135] Flacius, 69. Also see Flacius, 104. He writes:

> It is true, since our only Teacher Himself, the Son of God, repeatedly testifies to it, that no one is able to come to Him unless it has been given to Him by the Father, unless he is θεοδιδακτοι, that is, taught by God, unless the heavenly Father has granted Him revelation, yes indeed, unless He by His power draws us to Himself, who is undoubtedly the one font of true theology, as also of all other good works. We should therefore beg Him most fervently to inscribe in our hearts with His holy finger, namely the Holy Spirit, his law and knowledge of it, and also to grant us most graciously the fullest knowledge of the Holy Trinity and His mysteries.

[136] Hägglund, 318. Hägglund may be confused here. There is a reference to Christ opening the scroll in Rev. 5. Nevertheless, there is no reference to a key directly. There is a reference to Christ possessing a key in Rev. 3:7 which echoes Isa 22:22.

writes: "[i]t is the office of Christ to open Scripture to us and to illuminate our heart to understand the Scriptures (Luke 24:45). We all must receive of His fullness. That happens, however, when we come to know Him and apprehend Him through faith."[137]

This does not mean that if one believes in Jesus that one never has any trouble with the meaning of a text. There is a second sort of clarity having to do with the concrete grammatical meaning of the text.[138] Since the Spirit comes through the Word, knowing the historical-grammatical meaning of the text is essential for grasping the inner clarity. In this sphere of meaning, ambiguity only comes about because of our ignorance of grammar or perhaps historical uses of words. Luther states that if human beings knew the grammatical meaning of Scripture perfectly, then we would be able to understand external clarity perfectly.[139] As we have seen previously, Flacius also agrees that this sort of clarity exists with his emphasis on the literal and grammatical meaning. We will also see below, that his concern for the external clarity of Scripture is also expressed in his emphasis on the need for rhetorical criticism and the *loci* method.

As an aside, it is important to observe, this concept of the Bible's clarity corresponds to the anthropology that both Luther and Flacius share. Regarding divine things (inner clarity) humans are unfree and bound.[140] They are pass-

---

[137] Flacius, 67.
[138] AE 33:26, 28.
[139] AE 33:26.
[140] AE 33:64-70.

ive subjects to God's unilateral action of revealing the true meaning of the text. According to earthly things (external clarity), they are free and rational.[141] Consequently, they must diligently study the grammar and the original historical meanings of different words within their context.[142]

---

[141] AE 33:70.
[142] Flacius, 49-50:
> Interpreters, who indeed ought to be the greatest help to the unlearned for learning the Sacred Scriptures, often darken them more than they explain them, whether from ignorance or malice, as they introduce their own thoughts and dreams into Scripture, and affix to it a wax nose (as the impious Jesuits of Cologne blaspheme Scripture). Certain ancient writers obscure the Sacred Scriptures, both on account of ignorance of the language and of the things themselves. The more recent Sophists certainly do so at the same time both on account of ignorance and malice. What more pernicious confusion of the sense of the Sacred Scriptures can be devised, I ask you, than to introduce plainly philosophical and Aristotelian meanings into the Sacred Scriptures for the most important words, or rather things, such as sin, righteousness, justification, faith, grace, flesh, spirit, and the like? The meanings of such words are obviously turned on their head in this way, because they point someone to his own power, to his own person, and away from the proper profession of the one Lamb of God and His sacrifice, merits and works as the one way of salvation, and so they confuse him by their deception, because he sees them holding out and preaching Moses, and good works, and the merits of men.
> 3. Language is not something obscure. There are many causes for obscurity, though, concerning which I will soon speak, especially our lack of knowledge of the word. A word is indeed a mark or image of things, and a kind of lens through which we may contemplate the things themselves. Therefore, if a word is obscure, whether in and of itself or to our understanding, we are unable to comprehend the things themselves from that word without difficulty.

Flacius' concern for the literal sense and the external clarity also lead him to a concern for the rhetorical criticism and the *loci communes*. According to Flacius, texts must be understood on the basis of their overall "scope."[143] This means, he says, understanding the text is like the human body[144]:

> When you undertake the reading of a certain book, immediately in the beginning, as soon as possible, first take care to have the scope, aim, or intention of the entire writing continually and properly in mind, which for the most part can be noted in a few words, and is not uncommonly found right away in the title, whether it is of one piece, as when the entire writing is arranged in one body, or many pieces, as when the work has a number of parts that do not relate to one another.[145]

Here Flacius suggests a that one must take into account a rhetorical unity of the Bible and its various books. This is an emphasis one also finds in the works of Melanchthon and the biblical humanists in general.[146]

---

[143] See discussion in Hägglund, 321.
[144] Hägglund, 321; Kordić, 229.
[145] Flacius, 107.
[146] See Kees Meerhoff, "The Significance of Philip Melanchthon's Rhetoric in the Renaissance," in *Renaissance Rhetoric*, ed. Peter Mack (New York: St. Martin's Press, 1994), 46–62; Matthew DeCoursey, "Continental European Rhetoricians, 1400-1600, and Their Influence in Renaissance England," in *British Rhetoricians and Logicians, 1500–1660*, Dictionary of Literary Biography, vol. 236, ed. Edward Malone (Detroit: Gale, 2001), 309–43; Timothy Wengert, "Philip Melanchthon's 1522 Annotations on Romans and the Lutheran Origins of Rhetorical Criticism," in *Biblical Interpretation in the Era of the Reformation: Essays Presented to David Steinmetz in Honor of his Sixth Birthday*, ed. Richard Muller and John Thompson (Grand Rapids: Wm B. Eerdmans, 1996), 118-40.

For Flacius, the ultimate unity of Scripture is found in Christ. This is also true of the rhetorical unity of the Bible. The ultimate goal of the text is to teach the articles of the faith, in order to create faith in Christ. Therefore, rhetorically, the unity of the Bible is to be found inner unity of the articles of the faith (*analogia fidei*).[147] Flacius describes these teaching as being gathered together in the creeds as a sort of summary. This summary forms the most basic structure catechetical instruction.[148] Together, this inner unity of the articles of the faith forms the basis for the proper interpretation of the Bible:

> All understanding and exposition of Scripture takes place according to the analogy of faith, which is, as it were, a sort of norm of healthy faith or a barrier whereby, whether through an external storm or a inner impetuousness, we are kept from being dragged outside the fence (Romans 12:6). Everything, therefore, that is said about or from Scripture ought to be harmonious with this afore-

---

[147] See Hägglund, 320; Kordić, 228-9.
[148] Flacius, 77-8. He writes:
> After this chief distinction, it is also useful for the student to receive some sort of brief catechetical instruction, which Scripture provides for us. First, it puts forth a sort of creed [Symbolum] for us in the first three chapters of Genesis, concerning the one true God, creation, the fall, and redemption through the blessed Seed, which the creeds now repeat; then, through the Ten Commandments, in which God Himself has summarized the law in a simple way; third, in the Lord's Prayer and the words of the Sacraments. These chief parts of doctrine have always been held as a sort of convenient method of catechesis, although they were execrably obscured under the papacy (indeed, even if someone learned them, he was still for the most part ignorant of them, for he learned them, to be sure, in Latin).

mentioned catechetical summary, or articles of faith.[149]

Although Luther also makes reference to the concept of the analogy of faith (also using Rom 12:6 as the scriptural basis), the methodology presented here is primarily that of Melanchthon.[150] Later, this method would function as the basis for both Lutheran and Reformed scholastic dogmatics.

According to Melanchthon's theological method, clearer passages in Scripture could function in such a way as to illuminate more opaque ones. The most luminous passages in the Bible are those that together formed the articles of the faith or *loci communes* ("theological commonplaces"). These passages were individually referred to as *sedes doctrine* ("seats of doctrine").[151] The articles of the faith are connected to one another via an inner analogy.[152] This understanding of hermeneutics was possible because Scripture was understood to be the product of one author, namely, God the Holy Spirit. This meant that the logic of

---

[149] Flacius, 79.

[150] See AE 2:151. Also see criticism of this in interpretation of Rom 12:6 in J. P. Koehler, "The Analogy of Faith," in *The Wauwatosa Theology*, 3 vols., ed. Curtis Jahn (Milwaukee: Northwestern Publishing House, 1997), 1:221-268. A more valid basis for the concept of the analogy of faith can be found in 2 Tim 1:13: "What you heard from me, keep as the pattern of sound teaching, with faith and love in Christ Jesus" (NIV).

[151] See discussion of the *sedes* and the *loci* method in Muller, 1:177-81; And also Robert Preus, *Post-Reformation Lutheran Dogmatics*, 2 vols. (St. Louis: Concordia Publishing House, 1970-2), 1:35, 1:44-9.

[152] See description in Robert Preus, "How is the Lutheran Church to Interpret?," in Klement Preus ed., *Doctrine is Life: Essays on Scripture* (St. Louis: Concordia Publishing House, 2006), 187-9. Also see in the same collect, "The Hermeneutics of the Formula of Concord," 232-5.

the articles of the faith (*analogia fidei, typus doctrinae, regula fidei*) was not something arbitrary imposed on the text (as later liberal critics would claim[153]) but rather part of the text and its deepest structure.[154] By this method of studying the Scriptures, the inner and external clarity of Scripture were integrated with each other. By faith in Christ and the enlightenment of the Spirit, the *sedes doctrinae* (which were part of the external clarity) were understood in their proper place in relation to the chief article of the Christ and his gospel.

Lastly, Flacius accepts Luther's conception of how one practices the reading of Scripture. Basing himself on Psalm 119, Luther developed a threefold practice for the study of the Bible.[155] The theologian is to study the Bible according to a threefold rule of prayer (*oratio*), meditation (*meditatio*), and suffering/trial (*tentatio*).[156] This rule stands as the natural corollary of Luther's understanding of divine activity and human passivity mediated through the Word. Because law and gospel spoken through God's Holy Scriptures makes the human subject passive (first through their

---

[153] Hägglund, 320.

[154] Ibid.

[155] See good descriptions in Oswald Bayer, *Theology the Lutheran Way*, trans. Jeffrey Silcock, and Mark Mattes (Grand Rapids: Wm. B. Eerdmans, 2007), 33-6. *Luther's Theology*, 32-7; Reinhard Hiitter, *Suffering Divine Things. Theology as Church Practice,* trans. Doug Stott (Grand Rapids: Wm. B. Eerdmans, 2000), 72-76; John Kleinig, "Oratio, Meditatio, Tentatio: What Makes a Theologian?" *Concordia Theological Quarterly* 66, no. 3 (2002): 255-68; Pieper, 1:186-90; Martin Nicol, *Meditation bei Luther* (Goettingen: Vandenhoeck and Ruprecht, 1984), 91-101. Both Nicol and Bayer note the influence of monastic practices of reading on Luther's method.

[156] See Luther's brief description in AE 34: 285-288.

humbling by the law and then through the receptiveness of faith in the gospel), a fitting method for the study of the Scriptures is the practice of passivity and receptivity. Prayer makes us ready to receive the Word.[157] Meditation is a continuous deepening of receptivity through reflecting on what we have received in the Word.[158] Suffering/trial breaks down our pretences regarding our own wisdom and makes us ready to receive. Trial and suffering also test our understanding of what we have received. It teaches us to recognize whether what we have received is from God or from some other source.[159]

Flacius agrees with Luther's method, although he does not delineate the rule in the formal way that Luther does. Rather, in the *Clavis*, he mixes the threefold rule together with other rules regarding the study of Scripture. In discussing remedies for our difficulties in understanding the Scriptures he states in regard to meditation: "The fourth remedy is persistent meditation and study of the divine law. For "persistent labor conquers all," and nothing is difficult for the willing. And for that reason, our only Teacher, Jesus, urges us to search the Scriptures (John 5:39)."[160] This is followed by this admonition to prayer: "The fifth remedy is ardent prayer. Whatever indeed we ask, we will receive, and the Lord will in the end at the right time graciously open that which is closed to the one knocking. By the enkindled light of His Spirit, He will enlighten and flesh out

---

[157] Bayer, *Theology the Lutheran Way*, 43-50.
[158] Ibid., 50-9.
[159] Ibid., 59-65.
[160] Flacius, 64.

for us who are led by His hand that which is obscure."[161] Lastly, in another section, Flacius agrees with Luther that the Bible is understood best by those who are tested and suffer: "[a]ffliction gives knowledge (Isaiah 28:19). 'It is good that I am afflicted so that I might learn your statutes' (Psalm 119:71). Affliction and the cross are therefore very beneficial for understanding of God and His Word."[162] Hence by studying the Scriptures in this manner, Flacius and Luther bid us to follow the model of Jesus, the incarnate Word, who, prayed ardently, meditated on the Scripture, and finally suffered the cross. What is true of the supreme exegete, the Word of God Himself, should also be true of us, his members (Rom 8:29, 2 Cor 3:18).

Flacius' *Clavis* is a beautiful presentation of how the Scriptures are to be properly handled by faithful teachers in all ages. His work is a rich patchwork of the biblical insights as they were reaffirmed and expounded by Luther and Melanchthon. For this reason, Flacius' work was used throughout the period of Lutheran orthodoxy and inspired the work of faithful teachers such as Salomon Glassius, Johann Gerhard, and Wolfgang Franz.[163] The *Clavis* was used well into the eighteenth century when it was displaced by other, in some way perhaps less faithful books on hermeneutics.[164] It is for this reason that the availability of the *Clavis* in an English edition, like the present one, is such a wonderful boon for the life and health of the Church. The

---

[161] Ibid.
[162] Ibid., 69-70.
[163] Hägglund, 321-2.
[164] Ibid.

Church is only the Church to the extent that it faithfully harkens to the divine Word. The Church is ever, to paraphrase Luther, a creature of the Word (*creatura verbi*).[165]

---

[165] AE 36:107. WABR 5:591.

PREFACE

In the beginning of this second part of my Hebraisms, I have thought it most appropriate to put forward this compendium about the way in which one should become familiar with the Holy Scriptures. And although in all of this work hardly anything at all besides this is dealt with and taught, I would nevertheless like separately in one place to put forth, as in almost all works, the value of the work, and to do so especially here at the beginning of the universal rules. I indeed think it best that the readers first know what benefit they can derive from this treatise, whether from what precedes this or also from what follows, for in that way each learns with greater fruit, knowing why all that comes next is being instructed and passed on, and why they should make use of it. Then they also will be both refreshed from the long labor of the consideration of the preceding parts and invited to the consideration of what follows. The sure hope of a reward and the great usefulness indeed gladdens all and invites even wretched mortals to most serious labors. This treatise will also conveniently serve as a brief abstract or argument for all that follows, and no doubt provide, as it were, a sort of comprehensive synopsis by which things can be more clearly understood and more steadfastly retained, and become a sort of isagogical survey of all that follows.

CAUSES OF DIFFICULTIES IN THE SACRED SCRIPTURES

Aristotle learnedly says that the first step to understanding things is to observe those things that are doubtful. It will be useful, therefore, to review in the beginning the causes why Scriptures sometimes might be more difficult. Yet I am not speaking of a difficulty of such a kind as the adversaries dream up with extreme blasphemy of the truth —that it is impossible to perceive the true sense of that which has to do with all the necessary doctrines, and that everyone must therefore flee to the popes and their councils and decrees as the most infallible and irrefutable interpreters, which as tribunals of a sort are able to interpret them— but wherever by our own fault a word or the sense of it is not clear to us, as in many other writings. I am not saying these things in order to give an opportunity for the impious to slander the Sacred Scriptures, or to deter anyone from studying them, but on the contrary, to excite all the more careful diligence on the part of the readers, and, wherever difficulties are observed, much greater exactness after the remedies that I propose have been thoroughly learned. Indeed, by employing diligence and prayer, the most certain truth concerning everything necessary is able to be discovered in them.

1. The hearer, both the unteachable and also the despiser of such things, does not comprehend those things which are of God. To be sure, daily experience teaches that much, and indeed almost everything having to do with learning is situated in the hearer or learner. The naturally

gifted will perceive everything more easily than the slow learner. Likewise, we see that one progresses more quickly than another in knowledge or skill, whether because he is more suitable for it or because he is more inclined to it. So also, in sacred doctrine all men are by nature not only slow and stupid, but also absolutely inclined toward and cast headlong into the contrary sense. Not only unable to love it, strive after it, and know it, we also judge it foolish and impious, and are absolutely abhorred by it.

2. Interpreters, who indeed ought to be the greatest help to the unlearned for learning the Sacred Scriptures, often darken them more than they explain them, whether from ignorance or malice, as they introduce their own thoughts and dreams into Scripture, and affix to it a wax nose (as the impious Jesuits of Cologne blaspheme Scripture). Certain ancient writers obscure the Sacred Scriptures, both on account of ignorance of the language and of the things themselves. The more recent Sophists certainly do so at the same time both on account of ignorance and malice. What more pernicious confusion of the sense of the Sacred Scriptures can be devised, I ask you, than to introduce plainly philosophical and Aristotelian meanings into the Sacred Scriptures for the most important words, or rather things, such as sin, righteousness, justification, faith, grace, flesh, spirit, and the like? The meanings of such words are obviously turned on their head in this way, because they point someone to his own power, to his own person, and away from the proper profession of the one Lamb of God and His sacrifice, merits and works as the one way of salva-

tion, and so they confuse him by their deception, because he sees them holding out and preaching Moses, and good works, and the merits of men.

3. Language is not something obscure. There are many causes for obscurity, though, concerning which I will soon speak, especially our lack of knowledge of the word. A word is indeed a mark or image of things, and a kind of lens through which we may contemplate the things themselves. Therefore, if a word is obscure, whether in and of itself or to our understanding, we are unable to comprehend the things themselves from that word without difficulty.

4. Experience teaches that foreign language is always difficult for others, and the same is true for common speech, which experiences perpetual change over time regarding how people speak, read, and write, and later the research the experts do.

5. Old language is also unfamiliar to people nowadays. Those in Rome hardly understood the old linen books and the annals of the guild of priests, as Horace testifies, although it was still the same language. So also, Germans now do not understand what was written at the time of Charlemagne, although they are the same words, as one can see in Otfried's version of the Gospels.[166] The entire ancient manner of speaking and living is utterly confusing and difficult for people today.

6. How things connect and flow often causes the beginning and the end to become unclear. This particular kind

---

[166] Otfried wrote poetic versions of the Gospels in the latter half of the ninth century.

of disadvantage, that is, when the discourse does not wrap up one part before moving on to the next matter, but always leaves one thing hanging on account of others, was found especially among the ancients, as Aristotle testifies in *Rhetor. 3*. The book of Herodotus may be included among examples of this, as Aristotle himself says, although occasionally even with Paul the discourse jumps around into diverse matters. This matter will be given its own section in this chapter.

7. Diversity in the way of speaking of individual writings, and especially those of the New and Old Testaments (although all the books ought to be received as being by one author, as is the case) also brings with it no little impediment for the inexperienced reader, so that someone may indeed become very familiar with the manner of speech of one of those writings, yet at the same time not understand that of the others. Furthermore, that difference in speech is often seen to bring with it at the same time a different subject matter. For that reason, the Sadducees, and from the beginning all the Jews, supposed that the teaching of the prophets was different than that of Moses. So also, many Christians today also suppose that the New Testament speaks and teaches something different than the Old.

8. The speech is very figurative, and that in many ways. Much of it is in similes, allegories, types, questions, hypotheses, personifications, and similar forms, which not just anyone is able to understand and discern without having been forewarned.

9. It has many and various tropes, and employs them frequently, of which not a few are uncommon in other languages, especially with respect to particular examples, for they are of another kind, although the tropes or figures of every language may be reduced to the same name.

10. The Hebrews often mingled among each other a series of tropes, whether of the same sort, such as metaphors, or of different sorts, such as metaphors, metonymy, synecdoche, anthropopathisms, and similes.

11. They often have double or even triple tropes in one expression, as is demonstrated in its own rule, such as, *the hand of God touched me*, where first an anthropopathic metaphor from man to God is used figuratively, and then the hand represents its effect, namely, punishment.

12. From afar, they make use of far-fetched and stubborn tropes, such as, *to build up a man* or *religion*, or, *to put on Christ* or *cursing*.[167]

13. They often also fit them together in an awkward fashion, such as, *the virgin daughter of Zion is built up and planted.*

14. One encounters anacoluthon[168] and anapodoton[169] of words, discourse, senses, and matters. Very often it happens that the words, the construction, the form of the speech, or finally, the proposition or matter at hand, if ex-

---

[167] Psalm 109:18.
[168] A lack of verbal symmetry, as the thought of a passage does not proceed as the grammar led one to believe it would.
[169] A kind of anacoluthon in which the subordinate clause is left incomplete.

amined according to the Latin way, correspond little to the preceding, or not at all, but must simply be understood.

15. One encounters many substitutions of parts of speech and secondary definitions in the Hebrew language.

16. Various parenthetical thoughts and reduplications are frequently employed, which unless most diligently observed and attentively pondered, disturb the understanding and comprehension of the reading, so that one loses track of the train of thought and in his lack of comprehension is like one wandering about alone in the woods. It is not uncommon that even the diligent reader returns three or four times to the beginning and tries to observe the train of thought and still has trouble doing so on account of those difficulties.

17. A lack of books often hinders the reader, because one cannot determine or cast light on the use of an obscure word or phrase from somewhere else. In other languages, such as Greek and Latin, on account of the abundance of books, one can often from other writings shed light upon the authors' various ways of speaking or passages that cannot be understood or explained on their own.

18. Scripture is brief in its words and sentences, on account of which that saying of Horace is applicable, *"When I labor to be brief, I become obscure,"* since brevity produces inconvenience in every language.

19. They join together many conflicting meanings, senses, or matters at one time and in the same sentence, as I will show regarding ellipses and in the chapter concerning choppy style and other rules.

20. Many things are likewise little understood, especially when the language is very choppy, as I will demonstrate with many examples regarding ellipses.

21. A lack of forms of the verbs and of proper conjunctions for connecting them produces many obscurities, as also a lack of cases, which is easy to see from other languages. For the articles in this speech unfortunately do not distinguish the cases to much avail. Indeed, the same article often serves many cases.

22. A lack of the arrangement of the words, as when it may not be readily apparent how the words fit together, often obscures the speech, which an individual may resolve without difficulty.

23. Occasionally individual words, which are connected as though incidentally to the others, express entire sentences, the brevity of which, much like a foreign custom, easily burdens the inexperienced and sleepy reader.

24. Now and then it deals with one matter as though dealing with two, and, on the contrary, with two different matters as though dealing with one, as I will demonstrate elsewhere in this part with its own rule.

25. Often the speech is excessively laden with words and senses, so that for that reason it is not easily understood by the inexperienced reader what the principle senses are, what the secondary senses are, and how they go together, or in what order they ought to be understood, considered, and stored in the mind, as well as whether they ought to be employed in their proper use or an alien use.

26. There is a great liberty in the uses of words in this speech, which through various tropes are oriented in one place toward one sense and in another toward another. That often leads the less experienced into doubt or even into error.

27. Sometimes one word doubles the sense, as I will show in the rule concerning words, which beyond and contrary to their nature receive a certain movement.

28. Great is the abuse of syncategorematic[170] words, that is, of all those parts pertaining to a word that cannot stand alone as a word themselves, whether you consider their meaning or their connection. These hinges or links have truly caused much enlightenment and confusion, depending on whether they are applied dexterously or unskillfully. Not only, however, does their meaning vary in astonishing ways, but frequently they also at one time amplify, at another diminish, and at yet another do not relate to the matter at hand at all.

29. For Latin ears the whole interrelationship of the speech is harder. The words or sentences are not smoothly and meticulously lined up and brought together as with many other writers. Rather, sometimes they tumble down unevenly, tossed about and turned around with one another

---

[170] A term that has no meaning on its own, without connection with another word.

in a sort of turbulence. In that the Holy Scriptures resemble Thucydides[171] and Sallust[172] more than a little.

30. The construction of the speech is sometimes not continuous, but rather abruptly shifts in the middle of things, so that it ends differently than it began. *"As for this Moses who led us out from the land of Egypt, we do not know what has become of him"* (Acts 7:40).[173] The alteration of the form of speech will be addressed in detail in the chapter about repetition.

31. Sudden permutations of persons, times, circumstances, and numbers can confuse the message more than a little. They are, however, very prevalent in Holy Scripture.

32. Whoever writes about the sciences deals with things for the most part more or less in general, since, as it is said, concerning the individual thing there is endless debate and thus no knowledge or certainty. The discussion of Holy Scripture, moreover, is a blend of individual and the general. All individual things have circumstances, completely varied in their kind, according to which they are adapted, and also quite innumerable, on account of which the message is necessarily influenced, so that it is not always easy either to thoroughly examine things or grasp them where it is necessary, partly on account of the variety,

---

[171] An important Greek historian of Athens in the fifth century BC, his work influenced that of later historians. Lorenzo Valla produced a Latin translation of the work in the middle of the fifteenth century, and that is probably what Flacius had in mind.

[172] A fourth century philosopher and writer, he wrote *On the Gods and the Cosmos*, an instruction manual on paganism.

[173] The whole verse reads: *"saying to Aaron, 'Make for us gods who will go before us. As for this Moses who led us out from the land of Egypt, we do not know what has become of him.'"*

partly on account of the number, and then partly on account of the diversity of the things, persons, and places.

33. The subject matter of the Holy Scriptures is weighty, mystical, and heavenly. Wherever, however, matters are obscure and difficult, it is difficult to understand the author. We see that all more easily understand a history, even if it is roughly and murkily written, than a subtle and mysterious philosophical disputation, even if it is laid out in very clear order, pedagogy, and speech.

34. Nowhere are the things and the materials handled so closely in one place in a broad and methodical fashion that nothing is left to be desired. In general their approach is indeed rather a sort of blending or average of individual expressions, or aphorisms, and analysis, and comprehensive explanations of these things. The different ways of handing things are certainly diverse (as everyone knows), such as when individual sentences are recited incidentally or succinctly, such as in the case of the aphorisms of Hippocrates,[174] of Phokylides,[175] or the sentences of the seven wise masters,[176] which are similar to the Proverbs of Solomon, or when the matters or materials are put forth in a continuous string of speech, in complete and clear order. Everything is certainly clearer in this approach, not only on account of the order, but also on account of the more complete exposition of the things, since certain parts, or pas-

---

[174] Greek physician from the fifth century BC, familiar for the Hippocratic oath taken by physicians.
[175] A Greek poet from the sixth century BC, known for the maxims attributed to him.
[176] Medieval tales drawn from legends found in both Eastern and Western cultures.

sages, are brought to light by others more plainly and lucidly. The Scriptures, as I have said, are similar when they are seen to deal with familiar things, yet for the most part they are a sort of blend of that twofold sort of writing.

35. It is certainly not clear why God has handed down Scripture in a sentence by sentence and concise fashion in certain parts, so that it is written like imperial law. Perhaps it is because both have arisen out of the same circumstances or out of the treatment of them? For both, as one is wont to say, are certainly born of the worst morals of human nature and the devil, or certainly upon the occasion of the same. Or perhaps because they thus better serve their individual assignments? For the Scriptures are in a great part compiled out of individual inspirations, speeches, and letters, which are given for the removal and reforming of evil through the guilt and punishment of men put forth by God. And this matter, or method, does not lack most serious grounds, yet at the same time does bring forth a sort of darkness for the inexperienced. More, however, will be said about this later.

36. Often something obscure is put forth, and that sometimes is only one word that is attached to other words, as will be discussed in the chapter about the order of sentences.

37. Sometimes something is left out from the material set forth, and one thing wanders off toward another thing, until finally the discourse again returns back to the first thing. This manner of digression is explained further in the chapter concerning the order of sentences.

38. It is not rare for there to be progression from one thing to another, at one time subtle and at another obscure, and I will in its place address the clarification of this inconvenience with its own rule.

39. Arguments or rationales are not always clearly distinguished. Here and there they are mixed up among themselves or are connected with other things.

40. Ignorance of the context, or insufficient consideration having been given to it, to the conditions and circumstances of the matters upon which the apostles and prophets from time to time reflect in speaking, is a cause of confusion. Moreover, sometimes errors and deceptions, or the spirit of the hearers, or some scandal and danger, or certain other things are read into the discourse and the message is accommodated to that.

41. Oftentimes the things, places, and customs mentioned, to which the message alludes, or from which the metaphors and comparisons are taken, being unknown, obscure the message. That material is elaborated upon more thoroughly in its own section in this part.

42. General sentences are often pronounced with excessive explicitness, or absoluteness, or also with power, such as, *"I am able to do all things through Christ"* (Philippians 4:13), so that the papists say that each person can therefore fulfill chaste celibacy; likewise, *"Whatever you bind on earth shall be bound in heaven, and whatever you loose on earth shall be loosed in heaven"* (Matthew 16:19), and, *"So practice and observe whatever they tell you"* (Matthew 23:3), so that they say that everyone in every

way ought to obey the pope and the bishops without any exception, no matter what they teach or command. Why one must restrict such will be addressed in its own section and in its place.

43. Untrue grounds are often put forth as true, or certainly are not connected with their effects. That provides an occasion for erring for the inexperienced. That will be dealt with in its own chapter.

44. Law and promise, or gospel, appear to be in contention to the undiscerning. Their concord and distinction is the surest key to all of Scripture. Their concord, however, consists of this, that one ought to know that the gospel stands above the law and in that way gives the life that the law promises and yet is unable to give on account of the guilt and the vice of fallen men, who are unable to produce obedience. Having lost its primary office, it now serves as a servant to the gospel in working righteousness and life, performing only an auxiliary function, namely, revealing sins and the wrath of God, compelling men to seek medicine. In this way it serves as a schoolmaster to lead men to Christ.

45. The true and native use of the law is certainly stressed in many places in Scripture, even though it has come to naught now through our guilt, namely, to justify and vivify. The auxiliary use, which now is the primary use, is put forth very faintly in the Old Testament. That gives to most an occasion for error. But this will be dealt with in the little book entitled "Concerning the Veil of Moses."

46. The veil of Moses entails manifold obscurity, which I will expound upon in that little book, which has the same title as this part, which also has been published before.

47. It is a wonderful feat of the wisdom and providence of God that He has wanted to pass down His mysteries to us, so that, like the first revelation, subsequent enlightenments also should be expected only from His gracious hand and His ready benevolence.

48. As He Himself saw fit, God revealed His mysteries in the beginning more obscurely and then later more clearly. We must certainly admire that and hallow it, as necessity produced the obscurity in prior times. Although no new and immediate revelation has been given directly from heaven, and no new portion has been added to the biblical books, still no one who is reasonable and is a student of the truth can deny that the theology and light of the Sacred Scriptures enlighten all time as the morning light enlightens the midday.

49. God has said much in parables, because it has not been given to all to know the mysteries of God, and He Himself wants to reveal them to the little children and hide them from the wise according to His good pleasure, as the Lord Jesus Himself has testified (Matthew 11:25,26).

50. Many things have also been hidden from the pious, so that they investigate the Scriptures all the more ardently and strive for a clearer discovery. In these things we must therefore be attentive with our whole hearts, meditating

upon the law of God day and night, constant and fervent in prayer. Lord, increase in us the faith and the Spirit.

51. Finally, we must here certainly know God and His mysteries as in a riddle and imperfectly, though in the next life we will know Him perfectly and see Him face to face. Then at last will He be pleased to illuminate that which is incomplete here, with which we must now be content, just as a fetus, enclosed by God in the womb of the mother, is content with its fate even though it does not yet discern the shining sun.

REMEDIES

Being able to find salutary remedies for such obstacles and disadvantages and successfully communicate them to others is a pious and beneficial undertaking. That is what I will diligently endeavor to do in this work, just as other writers, who have applied themselves to illuminating the Sacred Scriptures with their educated words, have done. These difficulties are indeed not insurmountable, especially for the pious. The most gracious heavenly Father has supplied many salutary remedies for these impediments.

The *first* remedy to be sought before all else and with the highest zeal is certainly the only font of all good, the heavenly Father Himself, who draws us to the Son; and the Son, revealed to us from the bosom of the Father, who for us is the Door, the Truth, and the Way to the Father; and finally the Holy Spirit, whose particular gift it is to lead us into the whole truth, make us θεοδιδακτοι,[177] or taught by God, and supply us with genuine and salutary thoughts in all our study and effort.

The *second* remedy is specific instruction or certainly more fruitful knowledge of those things that are dealt with in Holy Scripture, provided by the pious and experienced servants of Christ. This certainly consists above all in an awareness of our sickness and subsequently also of the only Physician, Christ.

The *third* remedy is a solid knowledge of the speech of Sacred Scripture, to which end a certain help is also afforded to us through the good will of God, in which we will

---

[177] θεοδιδακτοι is used by St. Paul in 1 Thessalonians 4:9.

diligently strive to either level or alleviate every obstacle or difficulty and make things clear for the pious reader. Here indeed lies the primary source of the difficulty of Sacred Scripture, with which theologians have almost never wrestled with the highest diligence, in order to know the Holy Scripture itself and the text more completely, or to explain it in such a way to others. They instead were content to speak about things which are easier.

The *fourth* remedy is persistent meditation upon and study of the divine law. For *"persistent labor conquers all,"*[178] and nothing is difficult for the willing. And for that reason, our only Teacher, Jesus, urges us to search the Scriptures (John 5:39). And it is the way and nature of the truly pious to ponder with the highest dedication and desire the law of the Lord and to take it in hand day and night, so that they are instructed through the reading of good authors.

The *fifth* remedy is ardent prayer. Whatever indeed we ask, we will receive, and the Lord will in the end at the right time graciously open that which is closed to the one knocking. By the enkindled light of His Spirit, He will enlighten and flesh out for us who are led by His hand that which is obscure.

The *sixth* remedy is also here, as in every other science and art, real life experience, which certainly wonderfully illustrates and clears up more obscure concepts.

The *seventh* remedy, and certainly an extraordinary one, is the fact that similar things are very often repeated,

---

[178] *Labor omnia vincit improbus*, a popular Latin saying from Virgil's *Georgics*.

and what in one place is said either very succinctly or very obscurely is elsewhere set forth more comprehensively and more clearly. Augustine thus very rightly says that there is hardly any figurative sentence set forth that is not explained clearly elsewhere. The various passages of Scripture should therefore be dutifully compared. In this way, one will illustrate the other. In such an approach rests the most felicitous interpretation of Scripture, as the Father Himself also testifies.

The *final* remedy is good and clear translations and faithful interpreters of Holy Scripture, especially such who have more dexterously treated the text.

These matters are surely of the highest and greatest importance, and for that reason they will be treated throughout this entire work, and with that aim foremost in my mind, I will accordingly arrange the following treatise, in which I will present rules for the proper understanding of the Sacred Book.

I will first produce not a little out of Scripture itself, which will without a doubt be that which is the best and most certain. Then I will in another sequence review those rules which have either been demonstrated by others before or have occurred to me through the charity of the benevolent Spirit.

Lest the papists libel us as is their custom, I confess that the Scriptures present several difficulties, and that, no matter how many remedies I prescribe, they will still in no way be well-suited for the unschooled. For this reason, the inexperienced reader deserves to keep a distance from the reading of Sacred Scripture. One must recognize, however, that good translations, such as Luther's especially, have leveled most of these difficulties in countless places. Even though they do not express all the Hebraisms exactly and literally, they nevertheless more clearly and faithfully render the sense for us in our way of speaking.

Because the inexperienced to a great extent do not understand all the more obscure expressions of Scripture, yet in the meantime understand countless other places which speak more clearly, in which the same points are made, God gives to His Church faithful and learned ministers and teachers, in order to explain persistently the more difficult parts of Scripture in the public assembly and further urge and inculcate that which is already clear. Now let us return to our undertaking.

RULES FOR UNDERSTANDING THE SACRED SCRIPTURES, TAKEN FROM THE SACRED SCRIPTURES THEMSELVES

1. All good must be begged from God, especially this highest good, namely, understanding of the Word. For that reason, we may say with David, *"Open my eyes, that I may behold wondrous things from Your law... Hide not Your commandments from me!"* Therefore, proper understanding of the salutary and heavenly Scripture must be earnestly sought from God, through His Son. For to the one who seeks it will be shown, to the one who knocks it will be opened, to the one who asks it will be given.

2. It is the office of Christ to open Scripture to us and to illuminate our heart to understand the Scriptures (Luke 24:45). We all must receive of His fullness. That happens, however, when we come to know Him and apprehend Him through faith.

3. The Holy Spirit is at the same time the author and the interpreter of Scripture. It is His task to lead us into all truth (John 16:13). It is His task to write Scripture on our hearts (Jeremiah 31:33). For prophecies, and all of Scripture, as St. Peter attests (2 Peter 1:20), are not a thing of one's own intellect or interpretation, but rather as Scripture has been given by the Holy Spirit through prophecy, the same must of necessity also be interpreted in His light.

4. In Christ are all the treasures of the knowledge and the wisdom of God (Colossians 2:3). We dare not seek anything beyond or above Him. God will reveal nothing greater to us, as the Antichrist and the fanatics dream concerning

some greater mysteries, falling captive to foolishness and impiety on account of them and abandoning the others, even though Paul himself denies there is anything else to know than Christ crucified (1 Corinthians 2:2). Manifold, however, are the mysteries in the papacy: contemplation of angels, saints, and sacrifices, and especially monastic perfection, as well as Homeric descriptions of hell and paradise.

5. The ways of the Lord are right. The righteous walk in them, but the unrighteous stumble in them (Hosea 14:9). We must pay careful attention, therefore, so that we strive and learn to walk His ways and do not perilously stumble in them.

6. Not one jot or tittle will pass away from Scripture until all is accomplished. Rather, heaven and earth will sooner pass away (Matthew 5:18; 24:35). Therefore, one dare not despise or diminish anything in Sacred Scripture.

7. The authority of these doctrines revealed or pronounced externally and by God, through which God above all wants to deal with man, to teach and convert him, must in every way be defended. In this way God deals with man not as with an angel, but as with a corporal creature, so that through ears and eyes, in Word and Sacraments, yet still not without internal movement and illumination, He builds them up. For that reason, He instituted the external ministry and the Holy Book of His promises. And for that reason, He perpetually calls out and admonishes, so that we might listen. Paul has described this whole sequence of instruction and conversion step by step in Romans 10, verses 14

and 15, where he says that God sends teachers, namely, those having been instructed in the Sacred Scriptures and by the Spirit (Luke 24:45,49), to teach those hearing the Word of God from their mouth to believe, believing to call upon God, and finally, calling upon God to be saved. It is therefore the most plain masquerading of the devil when the fanatics, such as the Schwenkfeldians and popes, try to lead us astray from the Holy Bible to I know not what spiritual revelations and highly impure corners of their hearts, where all right and spiritual revelations are hidden away, although they are in reality a sewer of evil spirits.

8. The Sacred Scriptures must be read in the fear of God, so that we may stand securely and turn aside neither to the right nor to the left, whether in faith, in morals, or in any other actions (Joshua 1:7,8; Deuteronomy 5:32). For the fear of God is also the highest wisdom, so that it alone knows the right way and is heard in this, its house, as the one and only head of the household.

9. When we are converted to Christ, the veil is taken off our heart and also from the Scriptures, not only because we are illumined with spiritual light, but also because we grasp the scope and argument of all of Scripture, namely, the Lord Jesus, with His suffering and benevolent service (2 Corinthians 3:16). For the end of the law is Christ. That alone is the pearl of great price, and when we have found it in this field of the Lord, then we go about our life well satisfied.

10. Affliction gives knowledge (Isaiah 28:19). *"It is good that I am afflicted, so that I might learn Your*

statutes" (Psalm 119:71). Affliction and the cross are therefore very beneficial for gaining understanding of God and His Word.

11. It is useful right in the beginning to understand what one ought to get out of the proposed work, not only so that he might be more clear with respect to the work, but also so that he might recognize what to pluck from it and deposit securely in his heart. All that is written, therefore, is written for us, so that Scripture first binds us under sin and condemns us; then, testifies to us about Christ; third, consoles us so that we might have patience and hope; and finally teaches, rebukes, corrects, and instructs, so that the man of God may be perfected, equipped for all things (2 Timothy 3:16,17)

12. The highest, most constant and fervent effort must be applied to the learning of sacred things, for it is a characteristic of the pious to meditate upon the law of God day and night (Psalm 1:2) and diligently search the Scriptures (John 5:39; Acts 17:11).

13. It is beneficial to briefly set forth a summary of all knowledge of Scripture for those learning. The summary of Scripture, therefore, is these two syllogisms. The first and most important syllogism of the Old Testament is this: *Whatever God says is true.* That needs no proving. It is indeed the foundational principle of all theology, deserving of the assent of every creature. "Our words," say Moses and the prophets, "are the words of God, and He has spoken through us. Therefore our words and writings are most true, whether concerning creation and the fall, or the

blessed Seed and the Messiah." The lesser we may prove through the most miraculous exodus of Israel out of Egypt and their entry into the Promised Land; also through the subsequent chastisements, and the preservation of this people and their neighbors, the succession of the monarchs, and the other most manifest testimonies by which God, the author of such great works, has testified that this book and doctrine of ours is indeed His own. Further, the New Testament, reaping this syllogism of the prophets, this, so to speak, seed of theirs, builds up and closes out the syllogism of the old, the conclusion of the lesser assumed for the greater, as is accustomed to happen in preceding[179] and subsequent conclusions: *Whatever the Old Testament or the prophets have preached concerning the Messiah or other things, that is most true; or, Whatever description has been made about the Messiah by the prophets is most true. Our Jesus is indeed just such a person as the Messiah has been depicted to be by the prophets*, for He came at such a time as they described, namely, when Judah was no longer ruling to a great extent, in the time of the second temple, and at the end of the seventy weeks of Daniel. He also was born in such a place and from such a line as they described, and of a virgin mother. He also worked such miracles as they described, and was at the same time both God and man. He had such a one to prepare the way for Him as they described, and finally He died and rose. And so with His advent Moses and all the idols of the world fall to the ground.

---

[179] The conclusion in a prosyllogism is a premise to the syllogism coming before it.

Everything has by His coming at last come to pass, just as the prophets earlier preached. *Therefore this man Jesus is the true Messiah.* The lesser premise, which is a circumscriptive definition of Jesus, which is taken from various characteristics and circumstances, is born out through so many eyewitnesses: namely, not only the twelve apostles, but also the seventy disciples, the pious as well as the impious. Many things from this definition or circumscription of Jesus are attested also by the Jews and the Turks with their Koran, even to the present day, and those testimonies cannot be suspect. Some attestation is also provided by the ruins of Jerusalem itself and the dispersion of the rejected people, along with the abolition of its entire worship for so long.

With this second syllogism, which is peculiar to the New Testament, the first one, the syllogism of the Old Testament, is also borne out, that is, that whatever God says or testifies is most true of all. God by His testimony confirms the speech of Jesus, having three times spoken from heaven (Matthew 3:17; 17:5; and John 12:28), and He also makes His approval known through so many and such great miracles, concerning which the Lord Himself says, *"If you do not believe Me, at least believe on account of these works, which the Father works with Me"* (John 8:38).[180] And Nicodemus says, *"We know that You are a teacher who has come from God, for no one is able to do such things unless God is with him"* (John 3:2). And the

---

[180] The reference in the text is incorrect. This verse is actually John 14:10.

crowds said, *"When the Messiah comes, will he do greater things than these?"* (John 7:31). The destruction of Jerusalem, of the worship and the people here, may also be brought in here. Therefore, what Jesus and His apostles have said and taught is most true.

Having this summary of the entire Old and New Testaments in mind from the beginning, as it is contained in these two syllogisms, is most useful for a proper understanding of the Sacred Scriptures, just as it is beneficial for understanding anything any speaker says—a comedy or some other poem, history or book—to have an understanding of its argument or summary from the beginning, or as it is beneficial for understanding the parts or ages of world history to consider from the beginning the universal type and fasten it in one's mind. Indeed, when the human mind in the beginning briefly lays hold of the summary of a thing and then always keeps it in view, it is afterward much more easily able to work its way through the entire work, taking in the individual parts and comparing them with each other. The Evangelists supply us with this summary of the Old and New Testaments, and Christ Himself also does the same, as He so often repeats, *"This has happened in order that Scripture might be fulfilled."* In this way the hearer is warned concerning the minor premise of the aforementioned summary syllogism, and that is indicated to be the sum and scope of all Scripture, namely, as I have said, that such and such a person ought to be accepted as the Messiah according to the testimony of the prophets. Jesus is that person, which is patently obvious from here, there, and elsewhere in Scripture, and likewise from all the circumstances of His life. Jesus is therefore the true Messiah.

14. It is very beneficial for the reader right in the beginning of the reading of a writing to be advised about the scope and the kind of teaching, or material, that is dealt with in it, so that he may proceed as if guided by the thread of Theseus[181] and thus successfully and securely enter into, progress within, and exit out of this labyrinth, so to speak. For all longer writings, even those involving the most familiar material and produced in the best order and with clear language, are prone to trouble and confuse the simple and unlearned reader, on account of the range and the number of matters and senses contained within them. For that reason, one should quite appropriately fear for one who is in similar way inexperienced in Sacred Scripture.

Accordingly, it must be kept in mind that in this Book not only one kind of doctrine is contained, as otherwise is usually the case in individual books that are begun and constructed by one person, but two kinds of doctrine. And these are opposed to each other. The first says (according to Paul in Romans 10:5), *"Whoever does these shall live by them,"* that is, the most complete obedience of the law leads the one rendering it to eternal life. The other, however, contrarily cries out, *"Whoever believes,* or apprehends through faith that One who alone is able to fulfill the law and does so for the whole human race, *will be saved* (John 3:16). There are two kinds of doctrine, therefore: law and

---

[181] One myth concerning the life of Theseus, in legend the founder and first king of Athens, involves him making his way through a labyrinth by unwinding a ball of string as he traveled.

gospel. Both of these are indeed opposed to each other according to their nature. The former certainly offers salvation to none except those worthy and righteous. The latter, however, only offers salvation to the most unworthy.

They surely fit together in this way, that the one is higher than the other, for the law yields to the gospel, not only because it is inferior, but also because it is unable to perform the gospel's work, namely, salvation. That, however, is not its defect, but our own. The gospel, however, is able to do so. The law also yields not only in the office of justifying and saving the human race, but also stands by the side and is subservient in the perfecting function and work. Having lost its native aim and office, it does nevertheless perform a secondary service that God has marvelously apportioned to it. By nature its work, that is, in and of itself, was to give justification and life (Romans 7:10). Now, however, its secondary service or function, which, as it were, it alone performs now, is to reveal and accuse our most corrupt nature of its sins and at the same time pronounce the wrath of God and eternal damnation upon it. While it in this way accuses and convicts us of our sins and guilt of eternal punishment, it drives us to seek some Savior outside of us, and thus also compels us to flee into the net of the Messiah. In this way, it is the pedagogue to lead us to Christ. This is therefore the key to all of Scripture, or theology: to know that in it two kinds of doctrine are contained, and two ways of salvation, which stand in stark contradiction with one another, but yet agree with each other when the inferior yields to the superior, and in the place of its natural and original work or function now performs only an secondary function not native to it. It is as if there were in the same house two mothers, Sara and Hagar, who both wanted to rule and perform the highest office and therefore necessarily stood opposed to each other. But when the one yields to the other concerning the highest office, or grade of dignity, and humbles herself under her hand (as the angel commands in Genesis 16:9) and serves the same, things agree best between them. Paul illustrates this key of Scripture extensively in his Letter to the Romans and in Galatians 3 and 4, and hands it down and commends it to the reader who endeavors to enter into and inspect the Sacred Scriptures.

The papists and other deceivers, ignorant of this key, and forsaking the same, when they hear Moses and the law calling in Scripture, "Whoever does this will live by it," while Christ and the gospel call, "I have come to save sinners," they are right away troubled by these contradictory calls, or heavenly statements, and it is like they are tone deaf. Then, as if recomposing themselves, they reckon and decide that one must reconcile these two doctrines and doctors and somehow bring them into agreement by hook or crook. Without a doubt, they suppose, these two may be the same, and one sole doctrine thus contained in this Book, which on the one hand vehemently urges good works and on the other hand very much and shamelessly extols the grace of God and the merit of Christ. The sense, therefore, is certainly that we are saved partly through Christ and grace and partly through the law and works, or that through

Christ we receive the initial grace to enable us to perform the works of the law and be saved through it, or finally that we are indeed justified and saved through Christ first in Baptism, as in a safe and good ship, so long as we later perform no mortal sin, but if we do subsequently fall out of that ship by committing some sin, then it is necessary for us to have recourse to the second plank, to penance and good works, so that we may escape and evade the fate of a shipwrecked person. In this way they bring Moses and Christ, the law and the gospel, and grace and merits into agreement in three ways, or rather they confound them most abominably and impiously in three ways. When someone has recognized that, it will be most beneficial for his study of the Sacred Scriptures.

15. After this chief distinction, it is also useful for the student to receive some sort of brief catechetical instruction, which Scripture provides for us. First, it puts forth a sort of creed [*Symbolum*] for us in the first three chapters of Genesis, concerning the one true God, creation, the fall, and redemption through the blessed Seed, which the creeds now repeat; then, through the Ten Commandments, in which God Himself has summarized the law in a simple way; third, in the Lord's Prayer and the words of the Sacraments. These chief parts of doctrine have always been held as a sort of convenient method of catechesis, although they were execrably obscured under the papacy (indeed, even if someone learned them, he was still for the most part ignorant of them, for he learned them, to be sure, in Latin).

16. In every manner of teaching and learning, and every approach to it, whether in the liberal or mechanical arts, it is prescribed that we begin with the things which are beneficial for subsequent understanding, are easier, and contain, so to speak, what is in the end the sum of the thing. Such a manner of teaching also applies to the study of Scripture. The history is set forth first, which is ordinarily the easiest part, and then that history, especially the beginning of Genesis, serves as the foundation for all subsequent teaching about God and the entire true religion. Finally, those first three or four chapters of Genesis serve as a sort of summary of all of Scripture.

History is therefore presented first, which ordinarily is the easiest of all. Then that history, especially the beginning of Genesis, is the foundation for all subsequent teaching about God and the entire true religion. And finally those first three or four chapters of Genesis are a sort of summary of all of Scripture. There the one and triune God is presented, the creation of the universal nature of things, man, the worship of God in whose image he was formed, and the establishment of the Lord over all the world. Those things of which the first kingdom of God is constituted are presented there. It presents the law, the fall into sin and death, or the curse, and the guilt and punishment in which the kingdom of Satan lies. The blessed Seed and the restoration of the human race are then also set forth there. Finally, the beginning of this common life—marriage, procreation, labor, and toil—is presented. For that reason, the best approach to Scripture begins with these principles, for these are easier and are also the font and foundation of all teaching.

17. All understanding and exposition of Scripture takes place according to the analogy of faith, which is, as it were, a sort of norm of healthy faith or a barrier whereby, whether through an external storm or an inner impetuousness, we are kept from being dragged outside the fence (Romans 12:6). Everything, therefore, that is said about or from Scripture ought to be harmonious with this aforementioned catechetical summary, or articles of faith.

18. Christ often chided His apostles because they did not right away comprehend His speech, but were confused by certain words and especially metaphors, such as, for example, what the yeast of the Pharisees meant (Matthew 16:11), or the sword He assigned to them (Luke 22:28), or the sleep of Lazarus (Luke 22:28), or what food it pleased Him to eat (John 4:33). He therefore also similarly rebukes them in other places, such as when they do not understand the parable, or simile, of the seed, since they ought to understand all parables (Mark 4:13). In the final chapter of the Gospel of John, verse 23, they are reprimanded because they do not understand the question He asks, the pronouncement He makes regarding it, or the reason for what He said, when he said about John to Peter, *"If I want him to remain, what is that to you?"* They understood His reason for speaking and what He said on its face and affirmatively, that is, as if He had said, "I want him to remain," or, "He will not die." Christ therefore demands that we rightly understand both the meaning of the words used as well as

all kinds of tropes and figures, just as He also wants us to pay attention to the smallest jot and tittle, because none of the same will disappear or perish. So Paul also wants us to employ familiar and clear words in the church and in religious matters, especially in the presentation of doctrine and the exposition of the Sacred Scriptures (1 Corinthians 14:26). For this reason, Psalm 119:130 says, *"The unfolding of Your words gives understanding to the simple."* One must therefore exercise diligent care with the words of the Sacred Scriptures.

19. Further, Paul in 1 Timothy 1:7 wants us stick to and observe the nature of a proposition—what is the subject and what is the predicate, the definitions of the individual things involved, and the materials and arguments involved, whether of the entire writing or of an individual portion. He says, *"Deceivers pay attention neither to the things about which they speak,"* that is, whether something is a subject or an individual sentence or an entire discourse, *"nor to those things that they affirm or deny."* So, for example, there are those in our time who, when considering the freedom of the will, do not consider whether they are speaking about the natural or the divinely given will, or about the old or the new man, or also about how much the one is able to do on its own or together with the other. It is necessary, therefore, to distinguish carefully that about which something is said both from that which is affirmed or denied concerning it and everything else, especially all that is in its vicinity, whether in one sentence, discourse, book, or any other connection. Furthermore, we must know both

what it is that we are talking about and what it is that we are saying about it, and then also have definitions and clearly demarcated boundaries for the individual things, so that one is able to recognize already at the start (as Cicero has stated) what it is, strictly speaking, that the discourse is about. This indeed sheds the best light and provides the greatest help for perceiving the true sense of a certain passage, writing, or saying. Paul thus demonstrates with this statement that the vigilant teacher of the Sacred Scriptures and their hearers must recognize well the definitions of the words and matters involved, the subjects and predicates of individual sentences, and also the material, or subject matter, and purpose of the entire text and its parts.

20. He also wants the one explaining the Sacred Scriptures to rightly divide them (2 Timothy 2:15). That requires not only a solid understanding of the words, the meanings, the phrases, and the sentences involved, but even more of the individual members or parts of the body of a particular writing, which has to do with the entire arrangement of the books or writings, and certainly also with an exact distinction of those things, or materials, which are contained in the Sacred Scriptures, so that they are most carefully or accurately separated—the holy and the profane, the Creator and the creature, the righteous and the unrighteous, Moses and Christ, the doctrines and offices of both, etc. To this end, John makes a distinction right away in his Gospel between Moses and his teaching and the person and office of Christ. So also, Paul in Galatians 3 and 4 and Romans 3,4,5,6,7 and 8 distinguishes with the greatest care between the law

and the promise, or gospel, so that we are able to recognize what ought to be sought from and attributed to each, along with which is the inferior or superior doctrine, ruling the other or yielding to it, and what the proper use of each is with respect to the other, lest with the Jews and papists we should end up seeking righteousness and life from the ministry of sin and death, eagerly pursuing the righteousness of the law, or likewise transfer the ministry and doctrine of righteousness and life, which is the gracious promise concerning Christ, to the accusing, judging, and condemning law. The one teaching and studying the Sacred Scriptures, or *"word of truth"* as Paul here calls it, must therefore also properly and sufficiently distinguish both the word and the thing, as well as discern not only how disparate things differ from one another, but also how somewhat similar things might have differing parts, characteristics, elements, or specific circumstances, causes, effects and accidents, and in turn how many and very diverse things might become harmonious at times. Here the example of Plato certainly is useful: εφ εν και πολλα, that is, it is possible to discern and examine one thing in many things and many things in one.

21. The Apostle in Titus 1:9 also wants the teacher of Sacred Scripture to be fit for debating and rebuking the sophistry of deceivers. This includes not only the forms of true arguments and the fallacies of false arguments, as well as the materials and commonplaces of rhetorical invention, but also the entire field of language study and a firmer

grasp of individual definitions, propositions, and finally, things themselves.

22. He similarly in 2 Timothy 2:4 wants the expositor of Sacred Scripture to be apt to teach, which involves an understanding of the entire field of logic, or grammar, dialectic, and rhetoric, joined as well with a certain natural aptitude, which is much more splendid when the supernatural and supernal is granted by the Holy Spirit. We see that such a quality and instrument for the salutary reckoning and discerning of the Scriptures has been given to many from heaven.

23. Finally, he also in 1 Corinthians 14:40 commands, or rather the Spirit of the Lord does, that everything in the church and in religion should take place in an orderly fashion, especially the exposition of the heavenly doctrine, since God is not the author of confusion but of order. Certainly nothing is as ευχρηστον, that is, beneficial, as Xenophon attests and experience affirms, as a clear order of things. Now the way that order proceeds, that is, the way in which people come to comprehend things, is varied, which the teacher must keep in mind. On top of that, the Scriptures have their own particular order and sequence for presenting things, which the one teaching and the one learning must carefully note and observe. Most often, however, there are these three orders or methods: the synthetic, or compositive [*compositivus*], which Scripture for the most part follows; the analytical, or resolutive [*resolutivus*]; and the heuristic [*horisticus*], or definitive [*definitivus*]. And this is the second part of dialectics, less employed

today, about which I spoke in the *paralipomena*[182]. We have otherwise dealt with the method of the Sacred Scriptures elsewhere in this work.

24. It must always be properly observed that any genuine teaching must be obtained from the correct font. In the human sciences it is therefore appropriately prescribed that all methods and teachings must be deduced and built upon right principles in a proper and careful manner, and that they then should be confirmed through the nature of their subjects, experience, and the common good or benefit of men. Here, however, it is not our task to form or compose the kind [*genus*] of teaching, but rather we receive it already formed and composed in a book from heaven. What then remains is to learn to know it rightly and put it to daily use. The Son of God Himself, who alone reclines in His Father's bosom, has from there revealed all mysteries. To this font, therefore, or treasure, God sends us. These are our principles of this knowledge or wisdom, the κριτερια (criteria), or Lydian stone,[183] the norm for judging and the sermon book [*promptuaria*], as we heard earlier when He said, *"Search the Scriptures"* (John 5:39), *"To the law and to the testimony"* (Isaiah 8:20), and, *"They have Moses and the prophets"* (Luke 16:29).

25. Further, since some men send us off elsewhere for seeking truth, now to the ancients, now to the most learned ones, now to the fathers and the traditions of predecessors,

---

[182] Paralipomena are things added in a supplement to a work to address what may have been left out or not covered in sufficient detail.

[183] A touchstone. The ancients used a flint slate, or Lydian stone, to test gold and silver.

it is therefore necessary to carefully observe with respect to that that Christ and the apostles did not cite any fathers or their traditions or customs, which they no doubt would have been able to produce abundantly in their favor, in that way greatly increasing the respect that the Pharisees and priests had for their authority, as well as the respect of the people. They in fact produced no such thing, not the slightest either in their favor or contrary to it. Instead, they expressly found fault with the traditions of men. This demonstrates that all truth is to be drawn from the font of the Scriptures alone. We have been built upon the foundation of the prophets and apostles alone and upon that we must establish the church and the religion. We must strive to imitate and hear them lest we pay excessive attention to what men say, the traditions of men, and what kinds of rules or religions they might endeavor to command or set forth for us.

26. Christ says in Matthew 13:52 that every scribe who has been instructed in the kingdom of heaven ought to bring forth old things as well as new, as a head of household who out of his treasure is able to produce all kinds of food and other useful things. In this way, he shows that the expositor of the Sacred Scriptures ought to unpack the Old Testament together with the New and compare the old revelations, histories, and sanctions of God with the new ones, bringing them forth and explaining them publicly to others just as the apostles carefully did, comparing the words of the Old Testament with their own words. It also pertains to this that the Apostle said that all those things written in the

Old Testament serve as examples for us, having been written for our sake and not Abraham's (Romans 4:23; 1 Corinthians 10:6,11).

27. Christ's censure, that the Sadducees erred because they did not know the Scriptures and the power of God (Mark 12:24), must be carefully held in mind, for He thereby teaches that those piously and salutarily engaged in this study must bind God with His Scriptures, lest they believe Him to be something other than what He is, or to be laid hold of in some other way than that in which He Himself reveals Himself, lest they listen to the Scriptures other than as if God Himself were standing in front of them speaking, or doubt that all that God says and promises in Scripture is certainly as trustworthy and true, and in fact proceeds from the very mouth of God Himself, as if they were looking at Him standing there and listening to Him speak face to face with mankind.

28. Christ commands us to be on guard against the yeast of Sadducees (Matthew 16:6), because, as the Apostle attests in Galatians 5:9, even a little leavens the entire lump. So Paul also teaches from the Old Testament that we are to eat the Paschal Lamb without any leaven (1 Corinthians 5:7,8). Scripture concerning Christ, therefore, must be accepted even above every other article of faith and must sink into our hearts without the addition of anything from deceivers or philosophy, figments of human imagination or the traditions of men, and it must not be adulterated as happens with many when they mix certain works in with Christ (2 Corinthians 2:17). What does straw have to do with

wheat? What do the promises of God have to do with human dreams? (John 23:28).

29. In the exposition of Scripture and in the process of learning its true sense, after the gift of the Spirit of God, the comparison of similar portions of Scripture, whether similar in words, phrases, or subject matter, is the most effective tool. So also, such a comparison sheds light on an obscure sentence for us, as does the context, through a careful examination of what precedes and comes after it. So we read that Paul in Acts 9:22 confounded the Jews and proved that Jesus was truly the promised Messiah by drawing together the testimonies of Scripture and the prophecies of the prophets. Scripture is in every way a most rich treasure and the goodness and wisdom of God possessed in it is inexpressible, since nothing in it is so obscure that it cannot be explained or enlightened by the examination and comparison of other parts.

30. Scripture commands that those who study it possess burning zeal and diligence, particularly from the Holy Spirit, especially in the famous passage, Deuteronomy 6:7, where the Israelites are commanded to impress the Word of God upon their children, that is, not to suffer it to become rusty and dull, but to frequently and earnestly set forth before those listening the gravity of the righteousness, wrath, and law of God, and the severity of the Judge Himself. Thus Christ Himself with His sharp file, the Sermon on the Mount, removes in Matthew 5 and 6 the rustiness and dullness of the law produced by the Pharisees and their Pelagi-

an glosses. So long as any rust or dullness clings to or resides within the law, it is useless and ineffective for us.

31. One must in the Sacred Scriptures diligently observe and stay keenly aware of the scandal of what Paul calls the foolishness of preaching, with regard to which he says that he himself was the chosen instrument of Christ, having preached to the Corinthians in unrefined speech (1 Corinthians 1:21 and 2:1). Even more, he also confesses that he was not a skilled speaker, although knowledgeable in the subject matter. The earnest and manly eloquence of the Sacred Scriptures should not in the least be dressed up. It certainly lacks the leisurely and extravagant charms or allurements, the external sweetness and flattery, the abundance of tones or the trifling melodiousness, which are with longing and admiration heard and celebrated in the ostentatious writings of the orators or poets of that time in Greece and Rome. Even the matters themselves that are treated in the Holy Scriptures, although plainly divine, are utterly foreign to our intellect and likewise unrefined and perverted according to our own taste and way of thinking, easily offending us and thus quickly repudiated by us. For that reason, we must vigilantly be on guard lest we stumble, fall, and perish on this stumbling block, while we with the Greeks seek after that wisdom that is pleasing and acceptable to our taste (as Paul in 1 Corinthians 1:22 says of it) and are offended by the apparent foolishness of the preaching or teaching of divine righteousness.

32. In the beginning of his *Nicomachean Ethics*, Aristotle deals with the hearer or disciple of his teaching, in or-

der to show how and of what kind of disposition he ought to be when he wants to listen beneficially. In that way, the value of the work is demonstrated and something of its nature is made known to us by way of admonition. For proper instruction, then, not only a proven method of teaching is necessary, but also that the hearer be in the proper condition. He therefore desires that the hearer be fit and capable for his teaching. Now, this philosophy of ours binds and subjugates the hearer to itself much more, so that unless one first subjugates himself to it, reforms himself, and becomes suitable for the reception of its seed, there is clearly no true advantage or result to be achieved in the venture.

33. Philosophy wants right in the beginning to have a suitable and insightful listener. Our teaching, however, straightaway denies that any mortal is by nature suitable for perceiving it, because all men are creatures that do not perceive the divine. How should they not therefore, on account of the fact that their mysteries are absolutely divine and celestial, right at the start reject their despisers and all that have a most vexing hatred for the mysteries of God, who are called children of the world, who only speak about and have a concern for worldly things? There are thus no suitable disciples who come to Christ for teaching of their own accord, but rather only by the mercy and power of God are they drawn to Him and become θεοδιδακτοι, those taught by God (John 6:44,45). It is necessary for God Himself to prune and to illumine the hearts of those who otherwise have a heart not perceiving, eyes not seeing, and ears not

hearing. For this reason, this teaching wants its hearer to know in every circumstance that, despairing of himself, he must to beg God to open his eyes and grant him an aptitude for the achievement for such knowledge.

34. Scripture teaches that its mysteries are of such a sort that they are for the most part not understood by people in the highest positions and by the wisest, but instead are perceived, by the illumination of divine mercy, by the most foolish, contemptible, and lowly people. Christ gives thanks to the Father for this in Luke 10:21, and the Apostle affirms the same in 1 Corinthians 1:26,27.

35. These two teachings clearly coincide in that, just as Aristotle makes plain concerning ethics, the end goal is not to be knowledge but practice. With respect to this teaching, the end goal must be a hundred times more the same, for it is certainly far more impossible to restrict this teaching to theory without practice than moral philosophy.

36. Christ says in John 7:17, *"If anyone wants to do the will of the Father, he will know whether My teaching is of God or if I speak of My own authority."* With respect to this, Augustine rightly says, *"In theology you must believe in order to understand, not understand in order to believe."* In human sciences we certainly are convinced of something first and foremost through experience, through our senses and through demonstrations, before we grant assent. Here, however, it is exactly the opposite. We first assent or believe before we experience anything or are convinced by our senses and demonstrations. Aristotle thus

correctly says concerning this matter, *"The student must believe."*

37. In any science, and in learning in general, careful and regular exercises in that which has been already covered is very useful. So also, in the study of theology it is extremely beneficial to have a living practice of contrition, that is, a sense for one's personal sin, experience in and a sense for the remission of sin, or of justification and peace of heart, active consolations of the Word, the testimony of the Holy Spirit calling out *"Abba, Father"*[184] in our heart, varied and serious temptations, the manifold cross, frequent prayer, lamentations of faith in prayer, wrestling with Satan and adversities, a sense for newness, and eager and diligent study in obedience to God and pious living. It is therefore said very correctly in James 1:12, *"Blessed is the man who endures temptation,"* and in Sirach 34:10, *"What does the one who has not been tempted know?"* So also, Christ is said to have been *"tempted in every way, in order to sympathize"* (Hebrews 2:18; 4:15).

38. Here we should not despair if we do not grasp everything right away. The apostles and the blessed virgin kept mulling and storing up the sayings, sermons, and deeds of Christ in their memory all along, but only later did they first begin to understand them, at the arrival of an event, through an application, by the illumination of the Holy Spirit. Thus it is said in Luke 18:34 concerning the prophecy foretelling Christ's passion and resurrection, *"But they understood none of these things. The words were*

---
[184] Romans 8:15.

hidden from them. They did not comprehend what He was saying." On the contrary, it is said in verse 8 of Luke's last chapter that only then they remembered the things that He had preached and understood them.

39. In this comparison of the teaching of ethics and of theology the statement of Aristotle in *Ethics* 6 is particularly worth noting, that that the corruption of morals does away with the knowledge of ethics because it undoes the formal cause, that is, that all is to be suffered and endured for the sake of the grace of virtue and honesty. This is certainly one hundred times more true in theology. Where one actively gives himself to lust, avarice, and transgression, there he will not only suppose that he should suffer and endure little for the sake of piety and the glory of God, but the seven evil spirits, who do away with all true and pious knowledge and spiritual light, will also draw near to him, and he will become helpless prey for all darkness and such transgressions. One can certainly every day find fabulous, or rather terrifying, examples of this kind, even in the lives of great men, who are completely transformed. Even if sometimes such little men manage to say, "Lord," they nevertheless for the most part only mutter it with the mouth like a parrot and clearly babble contrary to their spirit.

40. According to their own manner the Sacred Scriptures contain a twofold knowledge concerning the same things. The one is, as it were, for beginners and little children, called through metaphor *"milk."* The other is for those already mature and strong, which is *"solid food"* (1 Corinthians 3:2 and Hebrews 5:13,14). The former is the

initial teaching of the chief parts of the Catechism, briefly, generally, and simply set forth. The latter is the subsequent teaching concerning the same things, but more carefully and fully presented, digging more thoroughly into the sources of things and expounding upon more abstruse questions and mysteries, which occur in those same parts. One must take care, therefore, that the less learned take in first that plain and simple milk toast and find comfort in it. The more robust, however, are to be led to that more solid food of more weighty doctrine.

41. There is a certain sort of disciple of Christ who always remains a child, as the Apostle reproaches the Corinthians, Galatians, and Hebrews. For these it is always necessary to have milk on hand. And another sort coincides with these, whom the Apostle describes in 2 Timothy 3:7 as *"always learning and never coming to the knowledge of the truth."* Their condition is perilous, to be sure. These are those who make no progress in learning, so that they become weak and daily begin to know less and less until finally all knowledge of the truth is completely extinguished in them. One must take up such who are sick in faith lovingly like a child and care for them with careful instruction, consolation, and prayer, in order to heal them. They indeed have a gracious Teacher, who has a learned tongue for teaching. He will not break the bruised reed or extinguish the smoldering wick.[185] Rather, He seeks out the weak sheep, bears them up on His shoulders, and carries them back to His herd and stall.

---

[185] Isaiah 42:3.

42. The end goal of this study, nevertheless, is the knowledge of God, the justification of the sinner, and the corporate worship of God. Just as Paul in 1 Thessalonians 5:9 says, *"We are appointed for salvation, not for destruction,"* so also we are said in 1 Peter 2:9 to be *"a chosen race, a royal priesthood, a holy nation, an acquired people, transferred from darkness into God's marvelous light, so that we may proclaim the goodness of the Most High."*

43. Knowledge in the Sacred Scriptures is also twofold: first, when God simply affirms or denies something, which is by far the most certain; and second, when we deduce something to be affirmed or denied from the expressions of God, in the process of which we can easily deceive ourselves. It is in this manner that the heretics most often have deceived themselves. Christ deduces the immortality of the soul, for example, from the expression, *"God is the God of Abraham, Isaac, and Jacob"* (Matthew 22:31,32), but for anyone else that would not have been such an obvious or foregone conclusion. So also, when the Letter to the Hebrews (8:5) expounds upon God's statement, *"See to it that you make the tabernacle according to the pattern that was shown to you on the mountain,"* such a conclusion would not have been in like manner so easy for us or evident to us.

Foolish men have always attempted to construct a third sort of theology, namely, by reasoning from philosophy or from certain other plausible propositions. The entire untheology of the sophists is of this sort. So also the Sadducees formerly wanted to refute the resurrection because so many possessors could not enjoy the same things which they had before possessed, whether wives, houses, fields, or other things; also because it would not be plausible either for their most holy fathers, who had handed down to them their traditions, to have erred or be damned, or for Christ to have become wiser than them, or for God to have permitted His people to have been in error for so long; also because Christ's teaching did not do much to extend discipline and gave an occasion for sinning. Along those lines, as then so now also the papists' innumerable sophists have reasoned, fabricating for themselves a sort of dream theology. So those who in this time maintain the synergism of the free will argue that it would follow from the teaching of damnation of the free will that God is the cause of the ruin of mankind and that negligence in an intention to undertake good works must result. Good God, what cries they have raised simply about favoritism [*prosopolepsia*]! Yet after one considers the matter, he sees that they have not even had a definition of favoritism. They have indeed said it is to give equally to those unequal or unequally to those equal. They have forgotten to add that in such things there is ultimately only favoritism when something is distributed on account of merit or debt, but that when someone acts of his own accord he is free to give liberally whatever and to whomever he wants, just as that great head of household says to his workers in Matthew 20:14,15. This kind of theology should therefore be shooed away as utterly vain and trifling.

44. Philosophies distinguish between knowledge and the knowable thing: the first sort, which are known of themselves, such as general principles and ideas, and the other kind, which only occur to us, such as common experiences and obvious things. Thus Paul in similar fashion praises the knowledge of God as something in and of itself plain and obvious to us, so that we are able to perceive what is hidden from His works and to enjoy His innumerable benefits in every hour, to reach out to Him and find Him, and to live and move and have our being in Him. But yet on account of the blindness of our hearts in sin the obvious God remains the unknown God for us, and when we endeavor to seize upon Him through reason we err and He disappears from us. Romans 1:19ff.; Acts 14:17 and 17:23ff.

45. In this study it is customary, as also in all other studies, for a pious teacher or guide to be extremely beneficial, and even completely necessary, as the Ethiopian eunuch demonstrates in Acts 8:31, when he denies that he could understand Isaiah without a teacher. And Paul likewise says in Romans 10:14, *"How will they believe without a preacher?"* Wherefore, as it is said, the Son of God sits at the right hand of the Father in order to give us pious teachers. In this connection, teachers are commanded in 1 Corinthians 14:30 to stop, be silent, and listen if a revelation comes to another one who is sitting at the time.

46. Further, according to the command of Paul, we must avoid seeking to know beyond that which is necessary and has been written. Rather, we are to content ourselves

with the Scriptures and think soberly (Romans 12:3; 1 Corinthians 4:6). There are certainly many who are not content with the simplicity of Scripture and the revelation provided there and want to know more than God has revealed in Scripture, such as the complete description of heaven and hell that the adversaries have adopted from the heathen poets, from Homer and Virgil, which they nevertheless industriously have expanded and dressed up more than a little.

47. Some also bring into Scripture all kinds of subtle, useless, and inexplicable questions with which they merely entangle and perturb themselves and others, especially as they cannot answer them. For that reason, Paul severely restrains them in 1 Timothy 1:4 and 6:3,4; in 2 Timothy 2:23; and in Titus 3:9. Such are (as we now remain silent about the Sorbonnists) those who in this time object with countless scruples and questions concerning the true sense of the Lord's Supper and the bodily presence of Christ.

48. We must see to it also, on the contrary, that we soberly and religiously philosophize in the heavenly doctrine, and that when we hold to the pattern of sound words, both individual words and phrases, as well as the entire speech, method, and material, we flee in every way from extravagant vanities and novelties of utterance, such as those we see not only the sophists and Sorbonnists have engaged in with their monstrous quarreling instead of teaching, but also the fathers, who in their peculiar zeal for rhetoric have explained many things in an unnecessarily immoderate manner. Some things, for instance, they have incorrectly exaggerated, such as virginity, and other things

they have improperly disparaged, such as marriage. Paul deals with this sound manner of doing theology in 2 Timothy 1:13, as well as Titus 2:8 and 1 Timothy 6:20.

49. There is in Christian teaching a certain insincere sort of study and progression by which some people (as the Scriptures say) seeing do not see and hearing do not hear. Some certainly have knowledge in theory but not in practice. They identify and are able to heal the sickness of others but not their own. They see the genus, but not the species or individual, and much less are they able to see the circumstances which greatly influence matters, which sometimes completely change the case. We must therefore pray for God to illuminate us through His Spirit with true knowledge and with pure and living light, so that we are not only able to piously and salutarily recognize the splinter in others' eyes, but also see our own plank and defect of any sort.[186]

50. Bad company corrupts good morals, and even the sincerity of faith, as Paul relates with respect to the article of faith concerning the resurrection in 1 Corinthians 15:33. One must therefore guard himself with all diligence against contact with the morally corrupt and impious, or with otherwise profane and impure writings, through which the Holy Spirit is grieved in the hearts of the pious, the strength of faith weakened, and true and ardent zeal cooled.

51. Our speech should always be salted with the Word of God, so that we and others are edified. No rotten chatter should proceed from our mouths, therefore, but rather what

---

[186] Matthew 7:3; Luke 6:41.

is commendable and edifying, so that our speech brings grace to others (Ephesians 4:29; Colossians 4:6). Finally, we are to be prepared always to give a reason for our faith (1 Peter 3:4). This is above all the end product to be sought and derived from this study.

52. The truth is everywhere the font of good, but especially in theology, as Plato also taught. On the other hand, error and falsehood are the font of evil. For that reason, Christ is called the King of Truth, who has come for this reason specifically: to propagate truth (John 18:37). On the contrary, Satan is the father of lies (John 8:44).

53. In every situation Paul's warning in Colossians 2:8, that we should be on guard not to be deceived through philosophy in the heavenly doctrine, is imperative. Here the Apostle speaks not only about pseudo-philosophy, but also about the abuse and fraudulent use of true philosophy. It is indeed impossible to describe how easily philosophy's propositions appeal to us and our foolish reason and ingratiate themselves into our thinking, mind, and conscience, so that we listen to them in the place of heavenly promises and follow them. Very often we mix, even completely unconsciously, the statements, precepts, dogmas, and consolations of the living God with the opinions of these insolent and shameless fancies of ours, bend and blatantly adulterate them, as if diluting the best wine in water. I have reviewed no trifling examples of these sorts of deception of philosophy in the handling of sacred things and sacred knowledge in the little book about the limits of the sciences. For that reason, we need especially in this regard the greatest

and most perpetual vigilance, God's help, and the light of the Holy Spirit, so that we most precisely and pronouncedly distinguish the holy from the profane. Our reason, therefore, the old Adam or human wisdom, should always be suspect to us in heavenly matters, and we should always diligently and attentively reflect upon heavenly revelations with complete watchfulness, on guard lest we even in the least depart from them.

54. Yet we dare not in this regard follow the fanatics, as if the human sciences were utterly useless or even detrimental to the knowledge of the Holy Scriptures and heavenly teaching. It is certainly necessary to study languages and well-informed grammars. Dialectic, rhetoric, and familiarity with the rest of philosophy is beneficial as well, and even quite necessary. Nor does the objection that the apostles did not learn the same carry water, because they received the knowledge of languages and other useful things by the gift of the Holy Spirit. We see many also today who, although otherwise unlearned, have been enlightened and granted an ability to resolve even the most obscure controversies with the greatest dexterity through a certain heavenly light of understanding. The Apostle therefore considers a knowledge of these external, or human, matters necessary for Christians, and especially for teachers, stating in Titus 3:14, *"And let our people also learn to devote themselves to good works* (or *functions) for necessary uses in order not to be useless."* There he has in mind especially their learning of the liberal and mechanical arts. So also, in 2 Timothy 2:2 he commands that theology be

committed to men who are apt to teach and learn, so that they are able to explain it to others. He in this way clearly considers the use of the logical sciences, or resources, necessary for students in theology. The philosophy of the gentiles should therefore relate in the household to theology as Hagar was to relate to Sarah. She is there to serve and be ancillary, not to domineer. She is not the lady of the house, but the handmaid. She may not enter into the chamber of the conscience or the tribunal for the judgment of sacred things, causes, or deliberations, except in so far as theology permits it, which is the lady of the house over all the sciences, arts, thoughts, counsels, endeavors, and actions of men and angels.

55. Investigation before instruction is beneficial. The student in this way sees for himself what he lacks and more eagerly receives the explanation of the teacher. Christ frequently makes use of this, such as when he as asks Philip, *"Where can we buy bread for these to eat?"* (John 6:5); or, *"How many loaves do you have?"* (Matthew 15:34); or all the disciples, *"Who do people say that I am?"* (Matthew 16:13); or Peter, *"Do the sons of the kings pay tribute?"* (Matthew 17:25). He does the same when He sets obscure parables before them, about which they were compelled to inquire when they realized that they could not understand them on their own. So also, He permits them to be vexed through their disputations with the Pharisees and exhausted through their unsuccessful attempt to cast out the evil spirit.

56. Examination after instruction is necessary. The student will in this way be more attentive, see what he lacks,

and also now be able to assess how correctly he has grasped the teaching. He will more diligently commit it to memory and, as if chewing on a cud, digest it. Christ frequently practiced this, such as when He asks, *"Who do you say I am?"* (Matthew 16:15[187]), or, *"Do you understand the parable?"* (Matthew 13:51).

57. But instruction is by far the most effective if applied not only through examination with words, but also with real life matters, so that students are compelled to put the teaching to real use and learn to swim, so to speak, without corks. Christ often does that with His disciples in the Gospels, such as, for instance, when, after the miracle of the feeding of so many thousands with so few loaves of bread, He took them along on a dangerous boat trip.[188]

58. Certain men today with gigantic audacity want to set what they have spoken above the authority of Scripture, and thus above God Himself, and interpret Scripture with utterly praetorical, or kingly, or, even better, tyrannical power, so that all are compelled to agree with their interpretations no matter how much they stand in contradiction with the text. Thus Cusanus[189] impiously blasphemes by claiming that the church and councils may interpret the same statement of Scripture now in one way and again in another, even contradictorily, and continue working in that manner as it sees fit. On the contrary, it is safest and at the same time most beneficial to explain and resolve doubtful or obscure Scripture through Scripture itself, so that God

---

[187] The text cites Matthew 18:1, which clearly is not correct.
[188] Matthew 14.
[189] Nicholas of Cusa, 1401-1464, a theologian, philosopher, and jurist.

Himself and His Word serves as the supreme judge and arbiter of every controversy or uncertainty. Thus Christ in this regard acted most cautiously when He disputed with the devil about where and when God in a proper sense should be expected to protect men, namely, not when they are testing Him, but rather when they go about their ordinary vocation, business, and way (Matthew 4:6,7); and when He was discussing with the Jews whether or not the Messiah is the Son of David, since He elsewhere is called David's Lord and is said to be seated at the right hand of God (Matthew 22:42 and following). The Apostle Paul does the same. Examples of this approach to study are the compilation of testimonies of Scripture he compiles in Romans 3 and 4, and in Hebrews 1 and 2, where he collects these testimonies in order to explain how Christ may be said to be glorified in the future and also to be lower than the angels in His humiliation, or exinanition.

59. This is in fact of first importance, and I have nearly forgotten it, namely, that men, on account of their perversity and the curiosity of their enmity toward God, want to recognize the truth through miracles, as the Jews again and again demanded that Christ give them a sign from heaven (Matthew 12:38; 16:1), or also to have recourse to consultations with the dead and apparitions (Isaiah 8:19). Abraham also told the rich man that men would not very easily be converted even if someone were sent to them from the dead in order to advise them with their best interests in mind (Luke 16:30). The prophets also denied that dead are to be consulted for the sake of the living, but

rather insisted that one must instead return to the law of God. Father Abraham also says that men have Moses and the prophets to whom they ought to listen. So also, Christ and Paul warn that many false Christs and prophets will arise, do wonders, and lead men astray (Matthew 24:24 and 2 Thessalonians 2:9). They also urge us to beware of apparitions of angels (Colossians 2:18), and teach that we should anathematize even angels from heaven should they teach anything different from the written doctrine of the gospel (Galatians 1:8,9). Under the Antichrist, however, the Scriptures being neglected and utterly buried, these two fonts of dogma have been almost exclusively utilized: miracles of every sort and innumerable apparitions. These were for the most part either completely counterfeited by swindlers or were indeed pure illusions and deceptions of devils.

60. It is true, since our only Teacher Himself, the Son of God, repeatedly testifies to it, that no one is able to come to Him unless it has been given to Him by the Father, unless he is θεοδιδακτοι, that is, taught by God, unless the heavenly Father has granted Him revelation, yes indeed, unless He by His power draws us to Himself, who is undoubtedly the one font of true theology, as also of all other good works. We most fervently, therefore, should beg Him to inscribe his law and knowledge of it in our hearts with His holy finger, namely, the Holy Spirit, and ask Him to grant us most graciously a most complete knowledge of the Holy Trinity and His mysteries.

GUIDELINES FOR READING THE SACRED SCRIPTURES ACCORDING TO THE MANNER OF JUDGMENT WE HAVE ASSEMBLED AND CONSTRUCTED

1. In every thought, effort, and dealing, especially difficult ones, and above all sacred ones, it is most useful to implore divine help for inspiration and aid in our undertaking, for blessing upon its end, that is, a felicitous outcome, and for growth and fruit through our labor.

2. Since, however, one must attend to every endeavor with a pious mind of good intention, it is therefore especially necessary in this regard for one to consider and keep in view the attainment of the true and genuine meaning of the Sacred Scriptures, with the desire to use it with the best faith for the glory of God, for your benefit, and for the benefit of others, especially the spiritual and eternal benefit, not for show or gaining lucre, and much less for opposing the truth, as the papists read the Sacred Scriptures.

3. The pious man must therefore venerate the Sacred Scriptures and study them with such awe that he conscientiously resolves, not to read a dead book, so to speak, and also not to study some sort of very holy, serious, or wise writings of men, but rather to listen attentively to the oracles of the living God Himself, with whom and in whose presence he is there dealing. God indeed is the author of this book, and He has produced it for the human race, as He wants always to speak personally with men through this book, to teach them about Himself, and to instruct them about their own eternal salvation.

4. In all truly difficult things and affairs, the mind is easily distracted and agitated by various cares and thoughts. In this study the mind should therefore be free of all cares and, as it were, strangling thorns, and be entirely focused on this work. The mind should especially be free of all depraved thoughts and perverse affections.

5. The reader should be content to lay hold of the simple and genuine sense of the Sacred Scriptures, and especially of the passage that he is reading at the time, and he should not chase after any kinds of shadows or eagerly pursue dreams about allegories or higher meaning [*anagogia*], except when there is obviously an allegory and the literal sense is otherwise unsuitable or absurd.

6. As soon as he understands something and has a grasp on the matter, the student of Scripture should press on further in meditation, so that he learns both the thing and the principle all the more fully and then applies it to the employment and exercise of faith, prayer, consolation, or the instruction of others, and morals.

7. When something that we cannot immediately grasp presents itself, we should not be annoyed by the prospect of examining it more diligently, considering not only the text and matter itself, but also consulting commentaries and inquiring of the learned and pious.

8. When we encounter something that we are at the moment simply unable to grasp, then we should merely commit to memory its place and words, hoping and waiting for the Lord graciously to make it clear to us on some occa-

sion. Indeed, nothing in Sacred Scripture is in vain, and nothing ought to be held in contempt either.

Now these three principles are, as it were, external and general; we will now speak about those that pertain more to the text itself.

9. When you undertake the reading of a certain book, immediately in the beginning, as soon as possible, first take care to have the scope, aim, or intention of the entire writing continually and properly in mind, which for the most part can be noted in a few words, and is not uncommonly found right away in the title, whether it is of one piece, as when the entire writing is arranged in one body, or many pieces, as when the work has a number of parts that do not relate to one another.

10. Second, strive to have a grasp of the entire argument, the main point, the summary, or short form. I call the argument that more full consideration, both of the scope and of the delineation of the entire body, in which oftentimes the occasion necessitating the writing is indicated, provided that is not obviously contained in the writing itself.

11. Third, you have to keep the division, or arrangement, of the entire book or work before your eyes, and observe very carefully where, so to speak, the head, chest, hands, feet, etc. are located. In that way, you can accurately weigh the nature of its body, how all its members are connected, and for what purpose so many members or parts are brought together in this one body—what the correspondence, harmony, and similarity of each of the members is,

whether with respect to each other, the entire body, or especially that chapter.

12. Finally it will be useful also to mark out all of that which is of one body in a table, in so far as the various members and the anatomy, or distribution, is concerned, so that thereby you will be able to perceive and comprehend the flow and spirit of that work, and better impress it upon your memory, having all the subjects under your eyes in synopsis, or, as it were, in one glance.

13. These four things—the scope, arrangement, orientation, and outlined synopsis—ought to be orderly, correct, and valid. When they are laid out in such a way, they offer much help. So also, on the contrary, if they are skewed, they lead the reader to err enormously. The greatest vigilance and cautious examination must therefore be exercised in these things.

14. Those four things bring several advantages. First, its scope and entire main point sheds great light on the individual parts and also on its expressions, phrases, and vocables, so that you can more clearly perceive their general sense and avoid confusion. For instance, whatever appears to contradict that whole scope and argument, or main point, is indubitably foreign and false.

15. The arrangement also helps, so that you can better harmonize individual parts with the main point and thereby take hold of a twofold benefit: you have a useful foundation for understanding the individual sentence and also perceive how that corresponds and fits with the main point.

16. Third, it is important for one to be properly oriented, so that you do not go about blindly like someone wandering in the forest or someone making a journey in the dark of night, perplexed about your current whereabouts and also about where you are going. You should always know where you are and where you are going, which way is east, west, north or south, how far or how near you are to a certain river, mountain, valley, or precipice.

17. Fourth, this outline will enable you to connect what precedes and what follows consistently and more profitably, providing valuable assistance for realizing and understanding the true meaning of the passage in which you are lingering and the full benefit that one can or should receive from it.

19 [18]. Finally, you will then also understand the entire work more clearly and firmly and retain it more securely in your memory. Whenever you need to make use of it, whether as a whole or in part, you will also be able to apply it opportunely.

19. Now because the benefit of this examination of the Scriptures is certainly both enormous and manifold, we will now add in writing still a few more precepts of this sort, especially pertaining to individual passages and those difficult sections or texts, so that we can resolve and investigate the entire work and all its parts more exactly and accurately, and finally (with the blessing of God) thoroughly come to know it. For (to confess frankly what I think), while many interpreters have up until now in their examination of the Sacred Scriptures learnedly discussed their in-

dividual passages or sentences, none, or at least certainly very few, have regularly made a careful examination of the text itself when explicating the Scriptures. They been even inconsistent in pointing out its argument and arrangement, and also in frequently comparing and connecting it most diligently with the entire body—its head and members. While inspecting, pondering, and illustrating individual passages, they have often not compared and applied each one most carefully to the rest, and especially to the head, and, what is more, to the entire body. This, however, must certainly be done with supreme care and often, if each passage's power, nature, and proper use is going to be truly and fully recognized and set forth. But now, as promised, let us add the rest of the precepts of this sort.

20. When an entire text is obscure for us, whether on account of the circumstances or words in play, it will serve us well, as we have already said, to consider both the scope and particular nature of the entire body, whether it is narrative or history, catechetical or a treatment of a certain doctrine, intended for consolation or reproof, the description of something, an oration, or something else along those lines. We have spoken elsewhere about the rules for the various kinds of sacred writings or books.

21. When we have taken note of the kind of writing with which we are dealing, we should then investigate further its individual parts or members, or, as it were, its subdivisions. When we have discovered and divided these, we should consider them in connection with each other and with the whole. It is certainly impossible for something to

be a sound writing and not exhibit a certain scope and, as we call it, a body of some sort, as well as certain parts or members that are attached to one another, to the entire body, and especially with its scope in some order, manner, or, as it were, proportion.

22. It will also be very beneficial to apply to an obscure place or to an entire writing the Lydian stone of the rules of logic, whether grammar, rhetoric, or finally, dialectic. Since these arts are indeed made known to us through the beneficence of God and lit from the natural light that is all the time over us, and since they conform with the nature of things and the order that God has assigned to them, and finally, since they accommodate themselves to the human ability for comprehension (as the Sacred Scriptures), they will necessarily be of great benefit to us in the illumination of the Sacred Scriptures, if we apply them piously and cautiously.

23. One must also ask, as I have already said, to what kind and body of all those various kinds of writings with which these arts deal, which are accustomed to occur in the life of men, in the treatment of things, and in human affairs, a specific sacred writing and its passages belong, so that perhaps a passage may be ascribed to a certain kind of speech, whether judicial, deliberative, demonstrative, didactic, or some other form of writing.

24. Where that is grasped, the position, the parts of speech, and the arguments should be sought and established. The places upon which the arguments are developed should be determined as well, and, according to the pre-

cepts of dialectic, both the order of the entire writing and the definitions and divisions within it should be examined and weighed, if they are present, and finally also the argumentations. It is sometimes useful to sum these up in brief syllogisms or other forms of dialectic. One must then seek out what kind of invention, arrangement, and elocution is present. One should see what has been assigned to things and what to men, or what is said about their cause, and what also agrees with human habit and practice, and in what manner the speech of divine majesty differs from human vanity.

25. It also provides no insignificant benefit if you put the writing into your own words, so that with your words, an anatomy of sorts having been performed, you delineate the flesh, that is, the adornment of amplifications, ornamentations, digressions, and similitudes, from the skeleton, only taking up at first those things that are, as it were, the bases of the whole, which sustain everything else that derives from them and is, as it were, accidental, which also by necessity clearly adhere to one another like bones bound by sinews.

26. The reader must certainly exercise primary and the greatest care to consider the principal and substantive sentences, in which the determination of the question put forth primarily resides. His secondary care must be to consider those that are, as it were, external, derivative, or accidental. It is not uncommon for a reader with open eyes, or a hearer, to be unable to discern those primary sentences on account of the abundance and excessive splendor of accidental

ones. When such an anatomy has thus been performed, one will soon discern what the principal thing is and how the individual parts fit together with one another, as well as what is external and accidental. He will also in this way ponder and examine in what way each of the two should be applied. Through such a written diagram things are more deeply impressed.

27. In this anatomical sketch, so to speak, you will be able to include both a brief sketch, or a short abstract or epitome, and also a more comprehensive paraphrase. You will also in the end be able to ponder and comprehend things most fully and usefully, as you will know to which words and sentences you want or are able to fasten aptly the appropriate things and senses and guard yourself most religiously, lest you twist something in their sense, add anything foreign, leave out something which ought to be taught, set something forth too sparingly, speak something not clearly enough, or on the contrary extol something too much or exaggerate. That is truly the first, if I may say so, and principal benefit of the anatomical sketch or paraphrase.

I have already warned earlier that the scope of the entire writing and the individual parts or places must be most carefully observed, for from so doing flows a wonderful light for understanding the parts of individual sayings. I will explain what I mean with an example. Concerning Luke 7:47, *"because she has loved much,"* many have disputed whether the remission of sins should be called the cause or the effect of the love. The papists want it to be the effect and we the cause. The conflict can be resolved very easily, however, if one inspects whether Christ there is explaining some things to the Pharisee and demonstrating their causes and effects, as if teaching a student eager to learn, or if He instead is making a particular point in order to oppose the false opinion of the Pharisee who held that little woman to be most contemptible, who was astounded in his swollen self-righteousness that Christ would have any interaction whatsoever with such a contemptible person. If He is simply a docile student, then that *"because she has loved much"* demonstrates that the love is the cause of the remission of sins. If, however, He is confounding the false opinion or thought of the Pharisee and making a simple assertion, then the particle contains the foundation and evidence of the forgiveness or justification having already taken place. It is clear that it is an assertion or confutation of the Pharisee. It is indeed one thing to set forth and demonstrate something in opposition to an adversary and another thing to teach an obedient and docile student and explain to him the causes and effects of a thing.

So also, we can from the scope easily understand, together with its neighboring verses, John 6:52, where they ask, *"How is He able to give His flesh to us to eat?"* The Jews there are not acting like a student eager to learn from Christ how to properly enjoy the benefit of His body, the blessing and the teaching of it, but rather they simply are rebuking Him as unbelievers for a manifest lie, as if He had spoken the greatest possible fallacy, namely, that He wants them to eat His body, and they are denying that He is bread that has come down from heaven and gives salvation, that is, true God and Savior. So also, when Christ among other things also says there, *"The flesh profits nothing, but the Spirit gives life"* (verse 63), and, *"No one comes to Me unless the Father draws Him,"* etc. (verse 44), He is not acting to teach them how to enjoy His benefits, merits, teaching, or body, but He is chastising their native unbelief, their rebellion and hostility, which they bear within them from the womb, which is so stiff-necked and powerful that they must not only be led, but, as it were, forcefully seized and dragged along kicking and screaming. It is one thing for a student eager to learn to ask someone whom he regards as a truthful teacher about something, and in turn for someone to teach and explain something to a disciple who wants to learn; it is another thing entirely to argue against and chastise a stubborn adversary.

So also, the scope must be kept in mind in the Lord's Supper and then the sense will be clear. In this way, dreams will not be propounded, nor merely bare types or shadows of future things be thought to be involved and prefigured in it, as formerly among the Jewish people. Rather, the Son of God Himself establishes His testament in this case, speaking to His beloved disciples, with whom He was in the habit of speaking clearly, or, if He spoke something obscure, explaining it soon afterward. What man in his right mind, therefore, does not recognize that Christ, when He establishes His testament, speaks most clearly and specifically to avoid leaving His heirs in doubt or contention? Christ there strikes a covenant between God and the human race by His blood. He in so doing confirms and binds us with the blood of His sacrifice, distributing it to us and soon after that offering it to God on His cross. From the scope, therefore, which is not merely to establish a bare type or shadow, or set forth some sort of dream, but rather to establish His testament with the clearest and most specific words possible and fix the His covenant unalterably, one can easily gather the true and genuine meaning. Just as the observation of the scope does much to illuminate the true meaning, so also does a careful comparison and harmony, so to speak, of the context. I have spoken about this matter earlier and I will also later speak further about it and explain it with examples.

God has certainly provided marvelously for our imbecility, so that the Sacred Scriptures are written with such a wonderful skillfulness and a consonant harmony that not only another book, or other writings, and different places may shed light on a passage, but that passage itself and its whole context illustrates and explains itself exceptionally, so that doubt is nowhere more felicitously addressed and explicated than through careful and God-fearing consideration of that particular passage in the light of the Scriptures themselves. Nowhere is any other author or writing to be found that has been executed with such skillfulness and symmetry.

Properly dividing the text marvelously illuminates the true meaning, just as it is in all of nature especially beneficial to bind what ought to be bound and to distinguish what ought to be distinguished. The following passages should serve as examples for us. In Luke 7:47, the expression *"because she has loved much"* has for many come into obscurity, because they have not bound together all that ought to be bound. They have only cited and considered those poorly rendered words, *"her many sins have been forgiven, because she has loved much,"* since these all are attached to one another. *"Wherefore I say to you, her many sins have been forgiven, for she has loved much."* By the principle, that is, the head joined together with the rest, it easily becomes apparent that it is not an exposition of something, or not meant to teach the Pharisee what the efficient cause of the forgiveness of sins in Christ is, but rather it is brought forward to counter his way of thinking—her sins were indeed forgiven. It is in this way an affirmation made in connection with her evidence, not merely an explanation meant to teach what is the cause and what is the effect. So also, in the Lord's Supper, if you distinguish the words of the Lord in the essence and in the fruit of the testament (just as Calvin also has distinguished in 1 Corinthians 11), you will cut off any occasion for sophistry. You will also avoid being carried off into its spiritual fruits in the first part, where only the essence of the Sacraments is handled, concerning which I have taught with more detail elsewhere. Countless examples of this could be produced.

    The papists and the sophists have sinned most grievously and perniciously against this precept. They have very rarely seen to the reading of the Sacred Scriptures, and when they have been read, have only plucked certain little sentences at their discretion and, even more, have connected them to each according to their good pleasure like a young girl gathering flowers in the meadow according to her will and whimsy and playfully weaving them together into a wreath or something else. So also, they have played in the Sacred Scriptures according to their heart's desire, seeing to it that, when the pure words of Scripture are indeed spoken, they nonetheless botch them together into a patchwork according to their own sense at the expense of the sense of the Scriptures themselves. This kind of most woeful and pernicious calamity, among the countless others which have gone on, must be carefully observed. In that way, we should apply all the more religious diligence, so that the sense of passages is sought out both from the scope of the writing or text and from the entire context.

www.ingramcontent.com/pod-product-compliance
Lightning Source LLC
Chambersburg PA
CBHW031256290426
44109CB00012B/603